PARTY FOODS
Snacks and Appetizers For Easy Entertaining

Revised Edition

Joanna White

BRISTOL PUBLISHING ENTERPRISES
Hayward, California

A **nitty gritty**® cookbook

Printed in the United States of America.

ISBN 1-55867-299-0

Includes material previously published as *Party Fare,* ISBN 1-55867-218-4

Cover design: Frank J. Paredes
Cover photography: John A. Benson
Food styling: Randy Mon
Illustrations: James Balkovek

CONTENTS

TIPS FOR SERVING PARTY FOODS

Appetizers, hors d'oeuvres, starters or nibbles — call them what you will. These dishes are not the main course, but tempting tidbits that should excite rather than satiate the appetite.

- If serving predinner appetizers, the cardinal rule should be: keep it light.
- If serving a "starter," an appetizer eaten at the table before dinner is served, be certain that the dish complements the rest of the meal you are serving.
- If serving hors d'oeuvres for a cocktail party or buffet, a variety of selections in a substantial amount is the ruling guide.
- If serving several small dishes at once, be certain that they complement one another. It is important to balance flavors and textures, hot and cold, raw and cooked, simple and elegant.

Overall, one of the most important rules is: choose your party fare so that you can enjoy time with your guests and not be tied to the kitchen. Planning is the key to a successful party.

PARTY FOOD GUIDELINES

- Nowadays, be more aware of healthy alternatives when planning your menu. Allow some dishes for vegetarians and vegans. Choose some low-carbohydrate alternatives to crackers or bread, such as using lettuce leaves to hold fillings.

- Be creative with colorful, unique vegetables and increase the amount of protein dishes such as patés, terrines or sates, as opposed to serving high-fat foods like cheeses or fried foods.
- Don't limit yourself to the old standby of onion dip — there is a myriad of dressings available in the stores that can be used for vegetable dips. Try ginger dressing with a side of toasted sesame seeds or honey mustard dressing with toasted wheat kernels.
- Nachos no longer have to be limited to only melted cheese. Try toppings such as spiced, shredded chicken, black beans, green tomatillo salsa and maybe a sprinkling of pepper-jack cheese for a healthier alternative.
- Instead of plain raw vegetables, try marinating vegetables with a flavorful oil and vinegar dressing or bottled marinade and grill to slightly charred. Serve with aioli sauce, mustard sauce or pesto for a change.
- Plan your menu for the time you have available. Prepare as much as you can in advance and write down all the last-minute instructions, so the final touches will not be forgotten.
- Always have back-up supplies like crackers or crostini, bottled sauces like pesto or flavored spreads and maybe canned shrimp or chicken to make quick appetizers in a pinch.
- Presentation is a keyword in entertaining. You can put a whole menu together from purchased foods from your favorite deli — but serve in beautiful dishes with unique garnishes and a creative background and your party will not be forgotten.
- Place overturned flowerpots, unopened paint cans or even large cooking pots on your table

and drape with cloth. This will allow you to arrange your platters, bowls or baskets on different levels to create interest. Make sure hot foods are accessible. Place flowers or unscented candles among the dishes to create mood.

- No matter how well you plan, try to prepare as much as you can ahead of time. I like to make garnishes the day before, cover and refrigerate. Then you can quickly add the finishing touches that make your presentation special.
- Serve a contrast of hot and cold dishes.
- Offer different textures served together, such as crisp vegetables or crackers with a creamy dip.
- Avoid being monotonous with flavor — for example, using mushrooms in every recipe.
- When serving hors d'oeuvres on trays, supplement with self-serve foods like spreads and patés. with bread, crackers or veggies.
- If possible, disperse food stations throughout the room to encourage socializing.
- Coordinate appetizers with the type of cuisine being served for dinner, such as dim sum before a Chinese meal, or tapas before Spanish cuisine.
- To prevent tea sandwiches and canapés from becoming soggy, spread softened butter or cream cheese over the bread before applying the filling.
- If guests are standing and holding a glass in one hand, consider serving only finger foods so they won't have to do a balancing act.

- If appetizers are replacing dinner, count on 10 to 12 per person, and offer at least 5 or 6 choices.
- A general rule for cocktail parties is to consider at least 6 appetizers per person per hour.

A PANTRY FULL OF PARTY FOOD

Prepared foods in jars, bottles, cans and packages can provide instant, delicious party fare for drop-in guests. A well-stocked pantry is the harried host's best friend.

anchovies: mash and mix with oil, butter or cream cheese for spreads

artichokes: marinated or plain; serve on an antipasto platter, or mix with cream cheese

breads: to dip and spread

capers: sprinkle on top of creamy spreads for piquant flavor

caviar: serve as a decorative garnish on many items, for those who appreciate it

cheeses: hard cheeses to shred and sprinkle over fillings on toasted bread; soft cheeses to serve with crackers or to make spreads

chips: a variety of potato chips, corn chips and bagel chips for dippers

chutney: add flavor to dips and spreads

corn tortillas: fry or bake into chips or make small filled tortillas from leftovers

crackers: an assortment to serve with dips and cheeses

deviled spreads: ham, chicken or beef, to spread on bread rounds or crackers

eggs: add chopped hard-cooked eggs to mayonnaise for spreads

fish: smoked or not, canned or frozen; serve on an antipasto platter or mix into spreads

green chiles: diced; mix into spreads or sprinkle on cheese dishes

horseradish: add heat to sauces, dips and spreads

mayonnaise: a quick, essential base for spreads

meats: a variety of sliced luncheon meats for an antipasto platter

mustards: a variety to make sauces, dips and to serve on breads

nuts: a variety to serve as is or to flavor with butter, sugar and/or spices

oils: a variety of flavors for frying, creating dips or spreading on bread

olives: a variety for serving as is; or chop and add to spreads

patés: canned or from the deli case to spread on crusty bread, toast or crackers

pepper jelly: serve over cream cheese with crackers

peppers: bottled pickled peppers to serve on an antipasto platter

pesto: mix with cream cheese for spreads

pickles: serve whole or chop and add to spreads and dips

piecrust, unbaked: make pastry shells by lining miniature or regular muffin tins or tart tins and baking at 350° until brown; fill immediately or freeze

pita bread: to dip; or to butter, sprinkle with herbs and bake for pita chips

puff pastry: make pastry shells by following instructions for piecrust, but prick pastry several times with a fork before baking

sun-dried tomatoes: serve on top of or mix into bread spreads

vegetables: cut up or bottled, marinated; use as dippers or part of an antipasto platter

vinegars: a variety of flavored vinegars for sauces and dips

water chestnuts: add crunch to dips and spreads

STORING PARTY FOOD

- Store all foods in tightly covered containers to prevent drying.
- Freeze foods in a single layer on a cookie sheet. Then, stack frozen foods between layers of waxed paper. Use airtight containers.
- If using bags for freezing, use only moisture/vapor-proof freezer bags.
- Glass containers with airtight lids are acceptable storage containers for appetizers.
- Tea sandwiches can be frozen as long as the filling ingredients can be frozen. Fillings made with butter or cream cheese are ideal for freezing.
- Don't freeze fresh vegetables, tomatoes, eggs, mayonnaise, salad dressings, aspics or mousses.
- Freeze baked pastry shells and toast cups separate from their filling in airtight containers.

FLAVORED NIBBLERS

PORTOBELLO MUSHROOM CRUNCHIES

Portobello mushrooms are a great substitute for meat products because they are flavorful and beefy. Use either rye breadcrumbs for a tasty and unique caraway flavor or substitute Japanese panko breadcrumbs. Honey mustard dressing can be used as a dipping sauce.

4 cups fresh rye breadcrumbs, or panko
   breadcrumbs
½ tsp. salt
¼ tsp. pepper

3 large eggs
12 oz. portobello mushrooms
4 cups vegetable oil
salt

If desired, sieve ground breadcrumbs to make a more uniform coating. Add salt and pepper to breadcrumbs and place in a large bowl. Beat eggs in a separate bowl. Cut mushrooms into ½-inch-thick slices. Dip mushroom slices in egg mixture, then into the breadcrumbs, pressing firmly to adhere crumbs. Heat oil to 350° in a deep-fat fryer or heavy saucepan. Fry mushrooms in small batches for 1 to 2 minutes, or until mushrooms are browned. Drain on paper towels and sprinkle with a little salt. Be sure to allow oil temperature to return to 350° before adding more mushrooms. Serve immediately.

Note: Mushrooms can be fried a few hours before serving then reheated in a 350° oven for about 10 minutes.

MARINATED OLIVES

This recipe gives American olives a Greek flavor. It also makes a great gift to give friends for the holidays.

1 lb. large black olives, pitted or unpitted
3 stalks celery, finely chopped
3–4 cloves garlic, minced
juice of 2 lemons

1 whole lemon, cut into small pieces
1 cup extra-virgin olive oil
1½ cups balsamic or red wine vinegar
2 tbs. dried oregano

Sterilize 2 pint canning jars by submerging them in boiling water for 15 minutes; remove jars and air-dry. Submerge lids in boiling water for 3 minutes; remove and air-dry.

Drain olives and, if unpitted, slit one side with a knife to allow marinade to penetrate. Mix celery, garlic, lemon juice, lemon, oil, vinegar and oregano with olives in a bowl. Pack mixture into sterilized jars, making sure liquid completely covers olives. Add a little water if necessary. Clean jar tops well and seal with sterilized lids. Let stand 2 to 3 weeks in a cool, dark place, shaking jars every few days. Serve with toothpicks and small containers for olive pits, if necessary.

BACON POLENTA BITES

Use these mini polenta muffins as a basis for endless vegetable and meat combinations. Try using black olives, tomatoes and feta cheese, or chopped salami, green onions and cheddar or hot pepper-jack cheese as alternatives.

6 slices bacon, finely diced
3 cups chicken broth
1 cup yellow cornmeal
½ cup (2 oz.) grated Parmesan cheese
½ cup (2 oz.) grated romano cheese
salt
3 oz. soft blue cheese
¼ cup diced green onions
½ cup grape tomatoes, quartered
¼ cup toasted pine nuts
3 tbs. finely chopped basil

In a small skillet, cook bacon on medium-high until brown and crisp. Remove from heat and transfer the bacon to paper towels to remove excess grease. In a saucepan over high heat, bring chicken broth to a boil and gradually stir in cornmeal. Reduce heat to medium and cook until mixture thickens considerably, about 2 minutes. Remove pan from heat and stir in Parmesan and romano cheeses. Stir in drained bacon, taste and add salt if necessary. Butter mini-muffin cups and spoon in about 1½ tbs. hot polenta mixture. Make an indent in the center with your thumb. Refrigerate until mixture is set, about 3 hours.

To assemble the bites: heat oven to 350°. Line a cookie sheet with foil, lift out polenta rounds and place on cookie sheet. Make sure indent is noticeable; if not, re-indent to create a small pocket for the filling. Evenly divide the blue cheese, green onions, tomatoes and pine nuts among the 24 tarts. Bake for about 5 to 7 minutes until tarts are warm and cheese is melted. Sprinkle with chopped basil and serve immediately.

VEGETABLE ANTIPASTO (GIARDINIERA)

Makes about 3 quarts

Make a large batch of this when the vegetables are at their peak to keep in the refrigerator year-round. Serve on a platter with a few fresh vegetables, such as green onions, and perhaps some slices of good salami.

8 carrots, peeled and cut into 3-inch sticks

8 stalks celery, cut into 3-inch sticks

2 small zucchini, cut into 3-inch sticks

2 red bell peppers, seeded and cut into ½-inch strips

2 green bell peppers, seeded and cut into ½-inch strips

1 small head cauliflower, broken into small florets

18 small pearl onions, peeled, or 2 medium onions, peeled and quartered

½ can (6 oz. can) pitted black olives

½ cup pimiento-stuffed green olives

5–6 cloves garlic

5–6 small hot dried red chile peppers

6 cups water

1½ cups white vinegar

2 tbs. salt

2 tbs. mustard seeds

1 tsp. celery seeds

2/3 cup sugar

Sterilize 5 or 6 canning jars by submerging them in boiling water for 15 minutes; remove jars and air-dry. Submerge lids in boiling water for 3 minutes; remove and air-dry.

Layer a mixture of vegetables and olives in sterilized jars in an attractive arrangement, packing tightly. Place 1 clove garlic and 1 chile in each jar. Place water, vinegar, salt, mustard seeds, celery seeds and sugar in a large pot. Over high heat, bring to a boil and boil for 3 minutes. Pour brine mixture into each jar until vegetables are covered. Clean jar tops well and seal with sterilized lids. Refrigerate for at least 2 weeks before serving.

MARINATED ASPARAGUS OR CAULIFLOWER

If desired, this brine can also be used for broccoli.

3 lb. fresh asparagus, tough ends removed
3/4 cup cider vinegar or balsamic vinegar
1 tbs. dried dill weed
1 tbs. sugar
1 tbs. salt
1 tsp. pepper
2 cloves garlic, minced
1½ cups chicken stock or vegetable stock

Cut asparagus into bite-sized pieces and place in a shallow pan. Mix vinegar, dill, sugar, salt, pepper, garlic and stock together and pour over asparagus. Cover and refrigerate for 24 hours, turning occasionally. Drain before serving. Provide toothpicks for serving.

GRECIAN ARTICHOKES

Serve these savory morsels with crackers or bread rounds. This dish can also be used as a vegetable side dish by leaving the artichoke hearts whole.

3/4 cup dry white wine
3/4 cup water
1/4 cup lemon juice
1/4 cup extra-virgin olive oil
2 bay leaves

1/4 tsp. dried thyme
salt and pepper to taste
2 cans (14 oz. each) whole artichoke hearts, drained and quartered
1 1/2 tbs. anchovy paste

In a saucepan over medium heat, mix wine, water, lemon juice, olive oil, bay leaves, thyme, salt and pepper. Bring to a boil, reduce heat to low and simmer for about 6 minutes. Remove pan from heat, transfer ingredients to a bowl, add artichokes and cool to room temperature. Cover bowl and place in the refrigerator overnight.

Remove artichokes from marinade and set aside. Pour marinade into a saucepan over high heat, stir in anchovy paste and bring to a boil. Reduce heat to medium and cook until mixture thickens. Spoon thickened mixture over artichokes. Cool to room temperature and serve as is or refrigerated.

SPICED MELON BALLS

This cool, refreshing appetizer takes minutes to prepare and won't fill up your guests before dinner.

1 medium honeydew or Crenshaw melon
1 large cantaloupe
2 tbs. lime juice
2 tbs. honey
½ tsp. ground coriander
½ tsp. nutmeg
fresh mint sprigs or lime slices for garnish

Cut melons in half and remove seeds. With a melon baller, form fruit into balls and place in a bowl. In a separate bowl, whisk together lime juice, honey, coriander and nutmeg. Pour over melon balls, stirring to coat melon. Cover bowl and refrigerate for several hours before serving. Garnish with mint sprigs or lime slices. Provide toothpicks for serving.

MARINATED GOAT CHEESE

Serve these flavorful cheese cubes with toothpicks alongside Greek olives for nibbling. This recipe can also be served sliced as a first course with crusty French bread, as an accompaniment to a salad or as a stuffing for chicken breasts. It is pretty garnished with something red, such as finely chopped red bell pepper, crushed red pepper flakes, chopped fresh tomato or minced pimiento.

¼ cup chopped fresh parsley
1 tsp. dried basil
1 tsp. dried thyme
1 tsp. minced garlic

½ tsp. pepper
1 tbs. finely chopped fresh chives
1½ cups extra-virgin olive oil
1 lb. French goat cheese, cut into cubes

In a bowl, mix together parsley, basil, thyme, garlic, pepper and chives. Heat oil in a small saucepan until just under the boiling point and pour hot oil over herbs. Let mixture come to room temperature and pour mixture over goat cheese in a shallow bowl. Cover bowl tightly and refrigerate for up to 3 days. Bring mixture to room temperature and pour off excess marinade before serving.

NOTE: Oil will turn cloudy and slightly solid when refrigerated. When brought to room temperature, it will turn clear and fluid once again.

CURRIED CASHEWS

Cashews have a natural sweetness that goes well with curry flavors. Almonds can be substituted for the cashews if desired.

3 cups roasted salted or unsalted cashews
¼ cup *Clarified Butter,* page 131
1 tsp. salt, optional
1½ tsp. curry powder
1 tsp. cumin

In a skillet over medium-high heat, sauté nuts in *Clarified Butter* until slightly browned. Add salt (if using unsalted nuts), curry powder and cumin and sauté, stirring constantly, until nuts are well browned. Transfer nuts to paper towels to drain. Cool slightly before serving.

TERIYAKI MIXED NUTS

The gentle flavor of these nuts can be enlivened by using 1 tsp. chopped fresh ginger in place of the powdered ginger. Use any type of nuts that suit your preference.

3 cups mixed whole shelled nuts
3 tbs. butter
1 tbs. soy sauce
2 tsp. lemon juice
1½ tsp. sugar
1 clove garlic, crushed
1 tsp. powdered ginger
salt

Heat oven to 350°. Place nuts on a cookie sheet in a single layer and bake until golden, about 8 to 10 minutes. Melt butter in a saucepan over medium heat. Stir in soy sauce, lemon juice, sugar, garlic, ginger and salt to taste. Add toasted nuts to saucepan and stir to coat with butter mixture. Return coated nuts to cookie sheet and bake for 6 to 8 minutes, stirring occasionally, until nuts are browned. Remove nuts from oven and cool slightly before serving.

CRISP PITA CHIPS

These crunchy chips can be flavored with an endless number of spices; use your imagination. Serve them with a dip or eat them like a flavored cracker.

10 pita breads
½ cup (1 stick) butter, melted
salt, optional
seasonings: dried herbs, spice powders or flavored salt blends
toppings: sesame, caraway or poppy seeds; grated Parmesan or Romano or bacon bits

Heat oven to 400°. For crisp chips, split pita breads horizontally, cut each round in half and each half into 3 wedges to yield 12 chips per pita bread. For chewy chips, do not separate pitas: Cut pita breads in half crosswise and cut each half into 3 wedges to yield 6 chips per pita bread.

Brush pita wedges with melted butter on both sides and sprinkle with salt, if using. Sprinkle one side of wedges with seasonings and/or toppings, if using (if making crisp pita chips, sprinkle items on the rougher side). Place chips on a cookie sheet and bake for 10 to 12 minutes, until slightly brown. Chips will become more crisp as they cool.

CHEESE STRAWS

The addition of ginger makes these treats special. They make great nibblers at a wine party. For a fancy presentation, hold straws on both ends and twist in opposite directions before baking. Serve at room temperature.

2 cups flour
1 tsp. ground ginger
1 tsp. salt
2/3 cup (1 1/3 sticks) cold butter, cut into small cubes
2 cups (8 oz.) shredded sharp cheddar cheese
1/2 cup sesame seeds, toasted
1 tsp. Worcestershire sauce
4–5 tbs. cold water

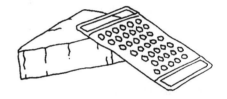

Heat oven to 400°. In a food processor workbowl or a bowl with a mixer, combine flour, ginger and salt. Add butter and cheese and process until blended. Add sesame seeds, Worcestershire and water, using enough water to form a stiff dough, and blend until dough forms a ball. Roll dough out on a floured surface to 1/8-inch thick and cut into 1/2-x-4-inch strips or "straws." Place straws on an ungreased cookie sheet and bake for 10 to 12 minutes or until golden brown.

SWEET AND HOT DATE-WALNUT WAFERS

Makes about 36 wafers

These popular treats can be frozen and brought out at a moment's notice.

2 cups (8 oz.) shredded sharp cheddar
   cheese
1½ cups flour
½ cup (1 stick) butter, softened
¼ tsp. cayenne pepper, or to taste
½ tsp. salt

¼ cup dry white wine
6 oz. pitted dates, chopped
1 cup walnuts, chopped
1 egg, beaten
ground walnuts, sesame seeds or grated
   Parmesan cheese, for garnish, optional

In a food processor workbowl or in a bowl with a pastry blender, mix cheese, flour, butter, cayenne and salt until mixture resembles cornmeal. Add wine and mix until moistened. Stir in dates and walnuts and form mixture into two 2-inch-diameter logs. Roll each log in waxed paper and refrigerate until ready to bake.

Heat oven to 375°. Cut logs into thin slices and brush slices with beaten egg. Sprinkle with toppings, if using. Bake for 10 to 12 minutes or until golden brown.

HOT AND COLD DIPS

WALNUT AND SUN-DRIED TOMATO DIP

This recipe can be used as a dip or a spread for sandwiches. Serve with toasted bread rounds, crackers, toasted bagel chips or tortilla chips. Toasted pine nuts can be substituted for the walnuts.

2/3 cup toasted walnuts
1/3 cup oil-packed sun-dried tomatoes, drained
3 tbs. bottled roasted red peppers, drained and chopped
2 tsp. diced green onions or shallots
2–2½ tbs. balsamic vinegar
3 tbs. water
1/3 cup extra-virgin olive oil
salt, optional

Place walnuts, tomatoes, red peppers, green onions, vinegar and water in a food processor workbowl or blender container and puree until well blended. With the motor running, slowly add olive oil until all the oil is incorporated. Taste and determine if you wish to add salt. Serve at room temperature.

CANNELLINI (WHITE BEAN) DIP

Makes about 4 cups

This dip is easy and can be made a day in advance. Cover and refrigerate until 1 hour before serving. Serve at room temperature with toasted bread rounds, tortilla chips or vegetables.

8 slices bacon, diced
1 medium onion, finely chopped
2 tbs. minced garlic
salt and pepper to taste
1 tbs. chili powder
1 tbs. cumin
2 cans (19 oz. each) cannellini beans

1¼ cups (5 oz.) shredded Monterey Jack or
   Gruyère cheese
½ cup sour cream
½ tbs. fresh lemon juice
½ tbs. fresh lime juice
cayenne or Tabasco to taste

In a skillet on medium heat, cook bacon until crisp and drain on paper towels. Reserve 2 to 3 tbs. bacon fat. Saute onions in reserved fat over medium heat until golden brown. Stir in garlic, salt, pepper, chili powder and cumin and cook for 2 minutes longer. Drain beans and rinse in cold water. Add to the onion mixture and cook 5 minutes. In a food processor workbowl or blender container, puree this mixture; add cheese, sour cream, lemon juice, lime juice and cayenne and blend until smooth. Taste and adjust seasonings. Reserve a few bacon bits for garnish and stir in the remaining bacon. Sprinkle top with reserved bacon pieces and serve at room temperature.

ROASTED RED PEPPER DIP

Makes about 2½ cups

Serve this dip with a beautiful array of fresh vegetables and garnish with fresh edible flowers and herbs. Look for whipped cream cheese in tubs in the supermarket's dairy case.

2 green onions, chopped
1 jar (15 oz.) roasted red peppers, drained
1–2 tbs. lemon juice
1 cup whipped cream cheese

In a food processor workbowl or blender container, process green onions until finely chopped. Add red peppers, lemon juice and cream cheese and process until peppers are coarsely pureed and ingredients are well mixed. Refrigerate until ready to use.

LOW-FAT CUCUMBER DIP

Makes about 2 cups

This refreshing dip goes well with vegetables or crackers.

1 medium cucumber, peeled, halved lengthwise and seeded
½ tsp. salt
⅓ cup low-fat or nonfat cottage cheese
1 cup plain low-fat or nonfat yogurt
1 tbs. chopped fresh parsley
½ tsp. dried dill weed, or more to taste
¼ tsp. white pepper, or more to taste

In a food processor workbowl or with a box grater, shred cucumber. Place cucumber shreds in a colander, sprinkle with salt and let stand over the sink for 30 minutes. Remove cucumber from colander and squeeze dry with paper towels. Process yogurt, parsley, dill and pepper in a food processor workbowl or blender container until smooth. Stir in cucumber, taste and adjust seasonings. Cover and refrigerate until ready to serve.

TOMATO SALSA

This is a must to serve with tortilla chips — freshly made if you've got the time. It's also good with bean dishes, vegetable salads and chicken. For a low-fat dipper, cut corn tortillas into wedges and bake in a 350° oven for 10 minutes or until crisp.

1 medium sweet onion, such as Bermuda, chopped
3 cloves garlic, minced
½ green bell pepper, chopped
½ red bell pepper, chopped
½ cup chopped fresh cilantro
2 tbs. lemon juice

2 tsp. sugar
2 cups fresh seeded and chopped tomatoes, or 1 can (15 oz.) Mexican-style stewed tomatoes
salt and pepper to taste
chopped fresh jalapeño pepper to taste, optional

Place all ingredients in a food processor workbowl or blender container and process with a pulsing action until just blended. Do not puree mixture; texture should be chunky. Taste and adjust seasonings.

GUACAMOLE

Save the avocado pit and bury it in the center of this mixture until you're ready to serve. This will help to keep the avocados from discoloring. Serve this dip with tortilla chips, corn chips, vegetables or tortillas wedges.

4 large, ripe Hass avocados, peeled and
   pitted, divided
juice of 2 limes
½ cup (4 oz.) shredded cheddar cheese
½ cup chopped Bermuda onion
1 pinch salt

1 jalapeño pepper, seeded and chopped,
   optional
1 tbs. chopped fresh cilantro
1–2 tomatoes, seeded and chopped
chopped fresh cilantro, for garnish

In a food processor workbowl or blender container, process 3 of the avocados until smooth. Add lime juice, cheese, onion, salt, jalapeño, if using, and cilantro and pulse briefly to blend. Taste and adjust seasonings. With a knife, cut remaining avocado into small chunks. Add avocado chunks to pureed mixture with chopped tomatoes and stir until incorporated. Place in a serving bowl and sprinkle with cilantro.

CREAMY AVOCADO VEGGIE DIP

Makes about 2½ cups

Offer a gorgeous array of crisp vegetables to serve beside this delicious dip. It also goes well with tortilla chips or crisp bagel chips. Try adding chopped black olives or tomatoes for a colorful twist.

1½ tsp. balsamic or red wine vinegar
1½ tbs. lemon juice
½ cup olive oil
1 tbs. Dijon mustard
¼ cup minced green onions, divided
1 tsp. salt
½ tsp. sugar

pepper to taste
8 oz. cream cheese, softened
2 cloves garlic, minced
1 large ripe Hass avocado, peeled and pitted
2 tbs. chopped fresh parsley

In a food processor workbowl or blender container, process vinegar, lemon juice, olive oil, mustard, 2 tbs. of the green onions, salt, sugar and pepper until smooth; remove mixture and set aside. Add cream cheese, garlic and avocado to machine and process until smooth and creamy. With machine running, very slowly pour vinegar mixture in a thin stream into cream cheese mixture and process until smooth. Transfer to a serving bowl and stir in remaining 2 tbs. green onions and parsley.

SWEET POTATO AND CARROT DIP

Makes about 4 cups

Dip into this piquant yet sweet vegetable dip with freshly cut vegetables or pita bread. You can steam the vegetables rather than boiling them to retain more of their nutrients.

1 lb. sweet potatoes or yams, peeled and
   cut into chunks
1 lb. carrots, peeled and cut into chunks
1 tsp. salt
3 cloves garlic

1 tsp. ground cumin
1 tsp. cinnamon
3–4 tbs. olive oil or vegetable stock
3 tbs. balsamic or red wine vinegar
1 pinch cayenne pepper, or more to taste

Place sweet potatoes and carrots in a saucepan over medium-high heat with salt and cover with water. Bring to a boil, reduce heat to low and simmer until vegetables are soft, about 15 minutes; drain. Puree cooked vegetables in a food processor workbowl or blender container. Add garlic, cumin, cinnamon, oil, vinegar and cayenne and process until blended. Taste and adjust seasonings.

GARBANZO BEAN DIP (HUMMUS)

This dip is quick to put together and is ideally served with fresh or toasted pita bread wedges. Tahini can be found in health food stores, Middle Eastern markets and some supermarkets. Add a few tablespoons of chopped chipotle chiles for smoky heat, if you like.

1 tbs. olive oil
1 small onion, chopped
2–3 cloves garlic, minced
2 cups drained canned garbanzo beans
½ tsp. turmeric

2 tbs. chopped fresh parsley
1–2 tbs. lemon juice, or to taste
2–3 tbs. tahini (sesame seed paste), optional
water, optional

In a skillet, heat olive oil over medium heat and sauté onion and garlic until soft and transparent. Rinse garbanzo beans with cold water and drain well. Place garbanzos, onion/garlic mixture, turmeric, parsley, lemon juice and tahini, if using, in a blender container or food processor workbowl and puree to the consistency of mayonnaise. If mixture is too thick, add a small amount of water.

SMOKY EGGPLANT DIP (BABA GHANOUSH)

This very healthy and tasty eggplant dip originated in the Middle East. The trick to this dish is in the smoky flavor obtained from scraping the charred eggplant skins. If you prefer a little heat, add a pinch of cayenne pepper. Accompany this dip with pita bread wedges or strips of Middle Eastern flatbread.

2 large eggplants, halved lengthwise
salt to taste
2 cloves garlic, finely minced
¼ cup chopped onion

lime or lemon juice to taste
1½ tbs. tahini (sesame seed paste)
2 tbs. chopped fresh parsley

Heat broiler. Place eggplants cut-side down on a cookie sheet. Broil eggplants for 15 to 20 minutes, until skin is blackened and flesh is softened. Remove eggplant from oven, sprinkle cut side of eggplant with salt and place eggplant in a colander to drain for about 15 minutes. Scrape flesh from eggplant skin, scraping some charred bits of skin into mixture for flavor. Puree eggplant pulp, garlic, onion, lime juice, tahini and parsley in a food processor workbowl or blender container until smooth. Taste and adjust seasonings. Refrigerate until ready to serve.

HOT GARLIC AND ANCHOVY DIP

This creamy variation of a traditional Italian dip goes well with freshly cut vegetables or bread rounds for dipping.

¼ cup (½ stick) butter
6–8 anchovy fillets, finely chopped
4 cloves garlic, minced
2 cups heavy cream
1 tbs. cornstarch
2 tbs. water

Melt butter in a saucepan over medium heat. Add anchovies and garlic and sauté for a few minutes, until garlic is soft and anchovies have melted. Add cream to pan and heat until just below the boiling point. In a small bowl, mix cornstarch with water and add to saucepan, stirring until thickened. Transfer to a heatproof bowl set over a candle warmer, or to a fondue pot. Serve immediately. Keep warm.

WARM SWEET PEPPER DIP

This quick, colorful, hot dip goes well with crackers, pita crisps or bagel chips.

8 oz. cream cheese, softened
½ cup (2 oz.) grated Parmesan cheese
1 small onion, diced
1 tbs. chopped fresh basil
1 red bell pepper, seeded and cut into chunks
1 green bell pepper, seeded and cut into chunks
1 yellow bell pepper, seeded and cut into chunks

Heat oven to 350°. In a food processor workbowl or blender container, process cream cheese with Parmesan until fluffy. Add onion and basil and process until mixed. Add peppers to cream cheese mixture and process until well mixed. Transfer to a shallow baking dish and bake for 15 minutes. Serve warm in a chafing dish or on a hot plate.

HOT CHEESE AND BACON DIP

This fast, delicious dip goes well with crusty French bread, breadsticks or crackers as accompaniments.

½ lb. bacon, cut into small pieces
1 can (8 oz.) tomato sauce
¼ cup finely chopped onion
½ tsp. minced garlic
⅛ tsp. pepper
¾ cup (3 oz.) shredded cheddar cheese, or 6 oz. processed American cheese cut into small cubes

Cook bacon in a small skillet over medium-high heat until crisp and transfer to paper towels to drain. Drain off most of the bacon fat from skillet and add tomato sauce, onion, garlic and pepper. Simmer for 5 minutes. Add cheese and stir until melted. Crumble bacon and stir into skillet. Transfer to a heatproof bowl set over a candle warmer, or to a fondue pot. Serve immediately. Keep warm.

SMOKY CHEESE FONDUE

Make this recipe with smoked cheddar cheese, smoked Swiss cheese or a combination of both — all variations are great. Serve with toasted bread cubes or wedges of pears and apples for dunking. For an additional treat, offer pieces of cooked bacon.

2 tbs. butter
2 tbs. flour
1 tsp. Dijon mustard, or more to taste
2 cups warm milk, or more if needed
3 cups (12 oz.) shredded smoked cheddar and/or smoked Swiss cheese
½ cup sweet white wine

In a fondue pot or nonaluminum saucepan, melt butter over medium-high heat. Stir in flour and mustard until bubbling. Add milk and whisk until thickened. Add cheese and stir until melted. Just before serving, stir in wine. Keep mixture warm in fondue pot, or transfer to a heatproof bowl and keep warm with an electric warming tray or candle warmer. If mixture begins to thicken, stir in a little more warm milk.

CRAB FONDUE

This delicious, creamy dip is best served with French bread rounds or plain crackers. Use enough paprika to achieve the color and flavor that you desire. Always be careful when adding any alcohol to a pan on the stove, as it ignites easily.

2 tbs. butter
½ cup chopped white or brown mushrooms
¼ cup cream sherry
salt and pepper to taste
1 pinch cayenne pepper
paprika to taste
1 cup heavy cream
3 egg yolks, beaten
1 lb. crabmeat

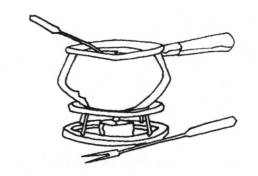

Melt butter in a skillet over medium-high heat and sauté mushrooms until tender. Carefully add sherry, salt, pepper, cayenne and paprika to skillet and stir to combine. Add cream and egg yolks to skillet and stir over medium heat until mixture thickens. Stir in crabmeat. Transfer to a heatproof bowl set over a candle warmer, or to a fondue pot. Serve immediately. Keep warm.

ORANGE MAYONNAISE DIP

Frozen limeade juice concentrate can be substituted for orange juice concentrate for a zesty alternative. Be sure to use grated lime zest in place of the orange zest. Sprinkle a few strands of zest on the sauce for garnish.

1 cup mayonnaise
3 tbs. frozen orange juice concentrate
1 tbs. toasted sesame oil
1 tsp. soy sauce
1 tsp. grated fresh ginger root
1 tsp. grated orange zest
salt to taste, optional

In a bowl, combine all ingredients except salt. Taste and determine if you wish to add salt. Cover and refrigerate until ready to serve.

CHIPOTLE HUMMUS

Chipotle is the new buzzword in the culinary world. A chipotle is a fully ripened and smoked jalapeño pepper. Tahini is sesame seed paste: both items are generally available in most supermarkets. Serve with toasted bread rounds, tortilla chips or bagel chips.

two 15 oz. cans garbanzo beans, drained
1/2 cup cold water
1/3 cup tahini paste
1/4 cup fresh lemon juice
2 tbs. extra-virgin olive oil
2 tsp. minced canned chipotle chiles, or to taste

2 large cloves garlic, minced
1 1/2 tsp. ground cumin
one 4 oz jar minced pimientos, drained
6 tbs. chopped cilantro
salt and pepper to taste

In a food processor, combine garbanzo beans, water, tahini paste, lemon juice, olive oil, chipotle chiles, garlic and cumin. Blend until smooth. Stir in pimientos and cilantro and taste. Add salt and pepper to taste and determine if you wish to add more chiles or seasonings. Chill until ready to serve.

SPREADS, MOUSSES AND PATÉS

FIG, OLIVE AND PINE NUT SPREAD

I like to serve this spread with softened goat cheese and toasted bread rounds. Regular black olives can be substituted for the Greek kalamata olives. I prefer Calimyrna figs, but any good dried figs will work well here.

1 cup chopped dried figs
6 tbs. water
½ cup chopped pitted kalamata olives
2 tbs. extra-virgin olive oil
1½ tbs. balsamic vinegar
1½ tbs. small capers, drained

1½ tsp. chopped fresh thyme
salt and pepper to taste
½ cup toasted pine nuts
diced red peppers or pimiento and/or
   chopped fresh thyme, for garnish

Remove the dried tough stems from the figs. Place figs and water in a saucepan and cook over medium heat until figs are soft and water is absorbed, 6 to 7 minutes. Remove pan from heat and allow figs to come to room temperature. Place figs, olives, oil, vinegar, capers, thyme, salt, pepper and pine nuts in a bowl, stir to combine and taste adjusting seasonings. Serve immediately.

Note: If you wish to make this ahead of time, withhold the pine nuts, cover and refrigerate until ready to serve. Stir in the pine nuts just before serving.

APRICOT SPREAD

Serve this sweet spread with tea breads. Or mix it with cream cheese to serve as a spread for mini-bagels.

1 lb. dried apricots
1 pinch ground anise
apricot or apple juice to cover
2 tbs. arrowroot or cornstarch
2 cups apple juice
1 pinch salt

Place apricots in a heavy saucepan with anise and add apricot juice to cover. Simmer over low heat until apricots are soft, about 30 minutes. Transfer mixture to a food processor work-bowl or blender container and puree until smooth; return mixture to saucepan and bring back to a simmer. Mix arrowroot or cornstarch with apple juice and stir into apricot mixture until thickened. Add salt, taste and adjust seasonings. Cool mixture and refrigerate until ready to use.

OLIVE SPREAD (TAPENADE)

This is a perfect dish to take to a party. Serve with thin baguette rounds or freshly made breadsticks. For a piquant twist, add a few anchovies with the capers.

2 cans (6 oz. each) pitted black olives
3 tbs. capers
½ cup minced onion
1 tsp. minced garlic
2 tbs. chopped fresh parsley
¼ cup (1 oz.) grated Parmesan cheese

2 tbs. olive oil
2 tbs. balsamic or red wine vinegar
1 pinch salt, or more to taste, optional
½ tsp. pepper, or more to taste
¼ cup chopped red bell pepper, divided

In a food processor workbowl or blender container, barely chop olives; transfer olives to a bowl. Place capers, onion, garlic, parsley, Parmesan, oil, vinegar, salt, pepper and 2 tbs. of the bell pepper in workbowl and process until minced. Transfer mixture to bowl with olives and stir until well mixed. Taste and adjust seasonings. Garnish with remaining red pepper.

SWEET PEPPER ANTIPASTO (PEPERONATA)

This healthy Italian appetizer has wonderful eye-appeal. Serve it with toasted bread rounds.

2–3 green bell peppers, halved and seeded
2 yellow bell peppers, halved and seeded
2 red bell peppers, halved and seeded
3 fresh tomatoes, diced
1 tsp. salt
1 tbs. minced fresh parsley
½ cup pitted black olives
2 tbs. capers or chopped anchovies, optional
2 cloves garlic, mashed

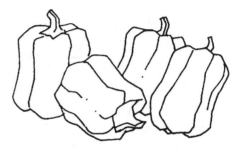

Heat broiler. Place peppers cut-side down on a cookie sheet and broil until skins turn black. Set peppers aside until cool enough to handle and peel off charred skin. Dice peppers and place in a bowl with tomatoes, salt, parsley, olives, capers and garlic; mix well. Refrigerate until ready to serve, stirring occasionally. Discard garlic before serving.

EGGPLANT ANTIPASTO (CAPONATA)

Makes about 6 cups

Serve this fresh vegetable spread hot or cold with rounds of crusty French bread. It can also be used as a vegetable side dish.

1 medium eggplant, peeled and diced
salt
¼ cup olive oil
1 medium zucchini, diced
1 large onion, diced
3 cloves garlic, minced
½ cup diced celery
1 large carrot, diced
1 green bell pepper, seeded and diced
1½ cups chopped tomatoes, drained

3 tbs. tomato paste
¼ cup chopped fresh parsley
½ tsp. dried basil
¼ cup red wine vinegar
2 tsp. sugar
¼ cup chopped stuffed green olives
¼ cup chopped pitted black olives
2 tbs. coarsely chopped capers
salt and pepper to taste

Place eggplant in a colander and sprinkle lightly with salt; set aside for about 30 minutes until some of the moisture has drained off. Heat oil in large skillet over medium-high heat and sauté eggplant and zucchini and until lightly browned. Stir in onion, garlic, celery and carrot and sauté for about 10 minutes. Add remaining ingredients, reduce heat to low and simmer gently for about 1 hour. Taste and adjust seasonings. Serve hot or cold.

CHUTNEY AND CHEESE SPREAD

Chutney and curry powder create a spicy, savory taste sensation. Serve this spread with crisp crackers.

8 oz. cream cheese, softened
1 cup (4 oz.) shredded cheddar cheese
2 tbs. brandy
1 tsp. curry powder, or to taste
1 jar (8 oz.) mango chutney
½ cup chopped toasted almonds for garnish
2 green onions, chopped, for garnish

In a food processor workbowl or in a bowl with a mixer, process cream cheese, cheddar cheese, brandy and curry powder until mixture is light and fluffy. Taste and adjust seasonings. Transfer mixture to a serving dish and cover with chutney. Refrigerate until ready to serve. Garnish with chopped almonds and green onions.

MOLDED HERBED CHEESE SPREAD

Shape this spread into molds to fit the theme of your party. Or, consider using it to stuff celery sticks or spread on small, shaped bread slices.

16 oz. cream cheese, softened
6 green onions, chopped
4 cloves garlic, minced
½ cup chopped fresh parsley
½ cup chopped fresh basil
1 tsp. dry mustard
1 tsp. Worcestershire sauce
¼ cup lemon juice
½ cup chopped black olives
salt and pepper to taste

In a food processor workbowl or in a bowl with a mixer, process all ingredients together until blended. Taste and adjust seasonings. Spoon mixture into an oiled 3-cup mold, cover and refrigerate until mixture is firm. To serve, invert mixture onto a serving platter.

GORGONZOLA SPREAD

This is a great spread to serve with toasted bread slices or thin pear slices. Gorgonzola is a creamy, pungent variety of blue cheese.

8 oz. cream cheese, softened
2 oz. Gorgonzola cheese, crumbled
2 tbs. butter, softened
2 tbs. chopped green onions
2 tbs. dry sherry
1/2 lb. bacon, cooked until crisp and crumbled, or 1/2 cup chopped toasted walnuts

In a bowl, mix cream cheese, Gorgonzola cheese, butter, green onions and sherry until well blended. Stir in bacon and refrigerate until ready to serve.

ROQUEFORT MOUSSE

This tantalizing spread is delicious served with an assortment of crackers and fruit. It goes especially well with sliced pears.

1 cup cold heavy cream
2 eggs, separated
16 oz. Roquefort cheese, room temperature
8 oz. cream cheese, softened

½ cup (1 stick) butter, softened
2 tbs. unflavored gelatin
¼ cup cold water
1 tsp. Dijon mustard

In a chilled bowl, whip cream until stiff and set aside. In another bowl, beat egg whites until stiff and set aside. In a large bowl, beat egg yolks until pale yellow, add Roquefort and beat until smooth. Add cream cheese and butter and beat until smooth. In a small saucepan, dissolve gelatin in cold water; gently heat mixture and stir until gelatin is completely dissolved. Add gelatin mixture to cream cheese mixture with mustard and stir until blended. Fold in beaten egg whites. Fold in whipped cream. Pour mixture into an oiled 7-cup mold and refrigerate until firm. At serving time, invert mixture onto a serving platter.

NOTE: If you are concerned about using raw eggs, increase cream to 1½ cups and substitute ¼ cup pasteurized eggs, such as Egg Beaters, for egg yolks.

BLUE CHEESECAKE

Serve this unique appetizer with rye bread rounds or crackers. Garnish with colorful edible flowers or carved vegetable flowers. Or, consider garnishing with a sprinkling of minced red bell pepper and green onions.

16 oz. cream cheese, softened
8 oz. blue cheese, crumbled
¼ tsp. white pepper
2½ cups sour cream, divided

3 eggs
½ cup chopped toasted pecans
¼ cup minced green onions

Heat oven to 300°. Butter a 9-inch springform pan. In a food processor workbowl or blender container, process cream cheese, blue cheese and white pepper until well blended. Add 1 cup of the sour cream and eggs and process until just mixed. Stir in pecans and green onions. Pour mixture into prepared pan and bake for 65 minutes. Remove from oven and let stand for 5 minutes. Spread remaining 1½ cups sour cream over the top of cheesecake and return to oven for 10 minutes. Cool completely and refrigerate overnight.

To serve, remove sides of springform and place cheesecake on a serving platter.

GOAT CHEESE, PESTO AND SUN-DRIED TOMATO TERRINE

Makes about 12 servings

This dish looks complicated, but it can be thrown together in minutes. It has beautiful eye appeal. Serve with crackers or sliced baguettes.

2 lb. cream cheese, softened
8 oz. goat cheese, crumbled
1 jar (8.5 oz.) oil-packed sun-dried tomatoes, drained
1 jar (10 oz.) basil pesto

In a bowl, mix cream cheese with goat cheese until well blended. Line a terrine mold or 9 x 5-inch loaf pan with a piece of wet cheesecloth. Spread ⅕ of the cheese mixture evenly in pan and cover with ½ of the tomatoes. Spread another ⅕ of the cheese mixture over tomatoes and cover with ½ of the pesto. Repeat layers, ending with cheese mixture. Refrigerate for several hours or overnight.

To serve, invert mixture onto a serving platter and remove cheesecloth.

SWEET AND SAVORY STUFFED BRIE

Makes about 24 servings

Serve this easy-to-fix appetizer with apple wedges and mild crackers. If desired, garnish with unpeeled apple slices and walnut halves. To prevent the apple slices from turning brown, dip them in a mixture of lemon juice and water.

1 large wheel (about 6 lb.) Brie cheese
2 medium golden Delicious apples, peeled, cored and chopped
1¼ cups brown sugar, packed
¼–½ cup crumbled blue cheese
1 cup chopped toasted walnuts

Heat oven to 325°. Slice Brie in half horizontally. In a bowl, combine apples, brown sugar, blue cheese and walnuts. Spread apple mixture on one cut-side of Brie and place remaining Brie half on top, cut-side down. Place filled Brie on an ovenproof platter and bake for about 20 minutes. Serve warm.

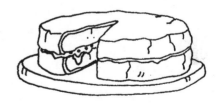

BRIE IN WINE ASPIC

Brie decorated in this fashion makes a really pretty, very impressive appetizer that will wow your friends. Serve with special crackers or rounds of French bread. Aspic is a savory jelly made from flavored liquid and gelatin. It is commonly used in French cuisine.

2 pkg. (¼ oz. each) unflavored gelatin
½ cup cold water
2 cups dry white wine
1 large wheel (about 6 lb.) Brie cheese
pansies or other edible flowers for garnish

For aspic, dissolve gelatin in cold water in a small saucepan; gently heat mixture and stir until gelatin is completely dissolved. Remove pan from heat and stir in wine. Let mixture cool slightly. Place Brie on a decorative serving platter. With a pastry brush, brush a layer of aspic on top and along sides of Brie. Artfully arrange flowers on top of Brie and gently brush with aspic. Refrigerate for 5 minutes in the refrigerator. Brush another layer of aspic on top (not on sides) of Brie and refrigerate for 5 minutes. Repeat brushing and chilling steps several times, until flowers are completely immersed in aspic. Refrigerate until ready to serve.

VEGETABLE-STUFFED BRIE

This beautiful, elegant treatment for Brie can be made ahead of time. Serve with rounds of crisp French bread or crackers.

1 large wheel (about 6 lb.) Brie cheese
2 cloves garlic, minced
1 small onion, chopped
1 tbs. butter
8 large white or brown mushrooms, finely
  chopped
½ jar (4 oz. jar) roasted red bell peppers,

chopped
1 can (4 oz.) sliced black olives, drained
1 tbs. dry sherry
salt and pepper to taste
chopped fresh parsley for garnish, optional
chopped red and green bell pepper for
  garnish, optional

Slice Brie in half horizontally and refrigerate until ready to use. In a skillet, sauté garlic and onion in butter until tender. Add mushrooms, peppers and olives and sauté for 3 minutes. Add sherry and season with salt and pepper.

One hour before serving, place one half of Brie cut-side up on a serving platter. Spread warm filling over cut-side of Brie and cover with remaining Brie half, cut-side down. If desired, garnish top of Brie with parsley or bell peppers. Serve at room temperature.

LATTICE CREAM CHEESE MOLD

This favorite spread is fancy enough to take to a party. For a change, use different complementary combinations of cheeses and meats. Serve with an assortment of crisp crackers.

FIRST LAYER

8 oz. cream cheese, softened
2 tbs. butter, softened
6 oz. smoked ham, minced
2 dashes Tabasco Sauce

SECOND LAYER

8 oz. cream cheese, softened
2 tbs. butter, softened
1$\frac{1}{3}$ cups ($\frac{1}{3}$ lb.) shredded sharp cheddar
    cheese
2 tbs. milk or cream
few drops orange food coloring, optional

THIRD LAYER

8 oz. cream cheese, softened
2 tbs. butter, softened
4 green onions, tops only, finely minced
few drops green food coloring, optional

GARNISH

4 oz. cream cheese, softened
sliced black olives
sliced pimientos

Line a 9-inch springform pan with plastic wrap. In a food processor workbowl, process first layer ingredients until blended. Spread mixture evenly in lined pan and place pan in the freezer.

In a food processor workbowl, process second layer ingredients until blended. When first layer is firm, spread second layer on top and return pan to freezer.

In a food processor workbowl, process third layer ingredients until blended. When second layer is firm, spread third layer on top. Cover pan with plastic and refrigerate until well set, at least 1 hour. When ready to serve, remove sides of springform and place mold on a serving platter; green layer should be on top.

For garnish, whip cream cheese until fluffy and place in a pastry bag with a small plain tip. Pipe thin stripes of cream cheese in a criss-cross pattern across the top of mold. Place black olives and pimiento slices at each intersecting line, alternating colors.

SIMPLE LIVER PATÉ

The traditional way to serve paté is to accompany it with cocktail onions, gherkin pickles and, of course, sliced crusty French bread.

1 lb. bacon
1½ cups chopped onions
1 lb. calves liver, cut into 1-inch cubes
1 lb. chicken livers, cut in half
2 tsp. salt, divided
1 tsp. pepper, divided
3 egg yolks
2 eggs
¼ cup Madeira or red wine
¾ tsp. dried chervil
½ tsp. dried tarragon
½ tsp. ground nutmeg
¼ tsp. ground allspice

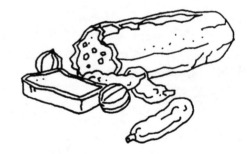

Line a 9 x 5-inch loaf pan or a 7-inch soufflé mold with all but 6 of the bacon slices. Dice remaining 6 bacon slices and cook in a large skillet over medium heat until browned. Add onions to skillet and sauté until onions are slightly browned. Add calves liver, chicken livers, 1 tsp. of the salt and ½ tsp. of the pepper and sauté until livers are no longer pink. Cool slightly.

Heat oven to 375°. In a food processor workbowl or blender container, puree liver mixture, a little at a time, until smooth. Add egg yolks, eggs, Madeira, chervil, tarragon, nutmeg, allspice and remaining salt and pepper to machine and process until well mixed. Pour mixture into bacon-lined loaf pan and cover with foil. Place loaf pan in a larger baking pan and add water until it comes halfway up the sides of loaf pan. Bake paté in water bath for 2 hours. Carefully remove pans from oven, remove loaf pan and pour off any excess fat; cool. Cover paté with a new piece of foil and place a weight, such as a brick, on top. Refrigerate for at least 8 hours before serving.

To serve, remove weight and invert paté onto a serving platter.

PATÉ WITH ASPARAGUS

This pork- and beef-based paté has asparagus dotted throughout. Serve it with crusty French bread and Asparagus Mayonnaise *to dollop on top.*

1 lb. ground pork
1 lb. lean ground beef chuck
1 cup fresh breadcrumbs
1 pkg. (10 oz.) frozen chopped spinach, thawed and squeezed dry
1 tsp. dried sage
1 tsp. dried thyme
2 tsp. salt
1 tsp. pepper
1 tsp. ground rosemary
2 cloves garlic, minced
1 tbs. chopped fresh parsley
6 spears fresh asparagus, tough ends trimmed
lettuce leaves, for garnish
chopped fresh parsley for garnish
Asparagus Mayonnaise, follows

Heat oven to 350°. In a bowl, thoroughly mix pork, beef, breadcrumbs, spinach, sage, thyme, pepper, garlic and parsley. Place meat mixture in a 9 x 5-inch loaf pan, arranging asparagus spears in a random pattern throughout. Bake for 45 to 55 minutes, until a thermometer reads 170° when inserted into the center. Remove paté from oven and cool. Cover paté with aluminum foil and place a weight, such as a brick, on top. Refrigerate overnight.

To serve, remove weight and invert paté onto a plate. Cut paté into slices and place on a serving platter lined with lettuce. Spoon a strip of Asparagus Mayonnaise down the center of paté slices and sprinkle with chopped parsley. Place remaining Asparagus Mayonnaise in a small dish to serve as an accompaniment.

ASPARAGUS MAYONNAISE

This can also be used as a dressing for pasta salads or as a spread for sandwiches. Or, it can mixed into a filling for deviled eggs.

¼ lb. asparagus, tough ends removed
1½ cups mayonnaise
¼ tsp. dry mustard
salt and pepper to taste

Steam asparagus until very tender, about 6 to 8 minutes; cool. In a blender container or food processor workbowl, puree asparagus until smooth. Add mayonnaise and mustard and process briefly, just until blended. Taste and adjust seasonings. Refrigerate until ready to use.

CRUNCHY HAM AND CHEESE BALL

Serve this ham-infused cheese ball with an assortment of crackers. Waiting until the last minute to roll the cheese ball in nuts preserves the nuts' crunchy quality.

8 oz. cream cheese, softened
1/4 cup mayonnaise
1 green onion, finely chopped
2 tbs. chopped fresh parsley
1/4 tsp. dry mustard
1/4 tsp. Tabasco Sauce
2 cups finely chopped cooked ham
1 cup chopped toasted walnuts

In a food processor workbowl or in a bowl with a mixer, mix cream cheese, mayonnaise, green onion, parsley, mustard, Tabasco and ham until blended. Form mixture into a ball, wrap with plastic wrap and refrigerate until ready to serve. Just before serving, remove plastic wrap and roll ball in nuts.

CREAMY CRAB SPREAD

Serve this stylish appetizer with plain crackers or bread rounds so that the delicate flavor of the crab can be fully appreciated.

3 hard-cooked egg yolks
½ cup (1 stick) butter, softened
½ cup mayonnaise
1 clove garlic, minced
1 tsp. Dijon mustard
1 dash prepared horseradish sauce

¼ cup minced green onions
¼ cup minced fresh parsley
12 oz. fresh crabmeat
1 tbs. fresh lemon juice
salt and white pepper to taste

In a food processor workbowl or blender container, process egg yolks, butter, mayonnaise, garlic, mustard, horseradish, green onions and parsley until smooth. Transfer mixture to a bowl and gently stir in crabmeat, lemon juice, salt and white pepper. Taste and adjust seasonings. Place in a covered container and refrigerate until ready to serve.

EASY CRABMEAT SPREAD

Makes about 2 cups

This quick, sophisticated dish goes well with crackers, crusty bread rounds or melba toast. If desired, garnish with a few whole crab legs.

8 oz. cream cheese, softened
2 green onions, finely chopped
2 tbs. lemon juice
¼ tsp. paprika
¼ tsp. white pepper
⅛ tsp. cayenne pepper
¼ tsp. salt
12 oz. crabmeat

In a food processor workbowl or blender container, process cream cheese, onions, lemon juice, paprika, pepper, cayenne and salt until smooth. Transfer mixture to a serving bowl and stir in crabmeat. Refrigerate until ready to serve.

QUICK SMOKED SALMON LOG

Makes 10–12 servings

This creamy "smoked" salmon spread can be made far in advance of serving it. Wait until about 1 hour before serving to roll it in the nut mixture. Serve with a variety of crackers or bread rounds.

8 oz. cream cheese, softened
1 can (16 oz.) salmon
2 tsp. minced onion
1/4 tsp. Liquid Smoke
1 tbs. lemon juice

1 tbs. horseradish
1/4 tsp. salt
1 cup chopped toasted pecans
2 tbs. chopped fresh parsley

In a bowl with a mixer, beat cream cheese, salmon, onion, Liquid Smoke, lemon juice, horseradish and salt until well mixed. Shape mixture into a log. (If mixture is too soft to form into a log, refrigerate for a few minutes before rolling). If not serving immediately, cover log with plastic wrap and refrigerate until ready to serve. Just before serving, mix pecans with parsley. Roll log in pecan-parsley coating and place on a serving platter.

LOW-FAT SALMON MOUSSE

For a pretty presentation, use a mold shaped like a fish or seashell. Surround the unmolded mousse with parsley sprigs and lemon slices. Serve with crackers or bread rounds.

2 pkg. (¼ oz. each) unflavored gelatin
½ cup cold water
1 cup boiling water
¾ cup low-fat or nonfat mayonnaise
2 cans (16 oz. each) salmon, drained
1 tsp. lemon juice
1 tbs. finely minced onion

1 tbs. Worcestershire sauce
1 tsp. salt
¼ tsp. pepper
8 oz. low-fat or nonfat sour cream
fresh parsley sprigs for garnish
lemon slices for garnish

In a small bowl, soak gelatin in cold water until dissolved. Stir in boiling water and cool until thickened. Beat mayonnaise into gelatin mixture until frothy. With a fork, break salmon into pieces, removing any pieces of skin or bones. Add salmon to gelatin mixture with lemon juice, onion, Worcestershire sauce, salt and pepper. Fold in sour cream. Pour mixture into a lightly oiled 6- to 8-cup mold, cover and refrigerate until firm. Invert mold onto a serving platter and garnish with parsley sprigs and lemon slices.

COLD FINGER FOODS

CHUTNEY-STUFFED CELERY

A delightful take on stuffed celery, this low-fat recipe has a spicy, sweet flavor.

1 bunch celery
8 oz. low-fat or nonfat cream cheese, softened
1 tsp. white vinegar
1 tsp. curry powder, or more to taste
6 tbs. mango chutney, finely chopped
1–2 tbs. milk
salt and pepper to taste

Separate celery into stalks, remove any tough strands and refrigerate until about 1 hour before serving time. In a bowl with a mixer, blend cream cheese, vinegar, curry powder, chutney, milk, salt and pepper to a thick but spreadable consistency. Taste and adjust seasonings. Stuff mixture into celery stalks, cut into 2-inch pieces and refrigerate until ready to serve.

STUFFED GRAPE LEAVES

Makes about 48 pieces

These Greek favorites are otherwise known as dolmades.

1 jar (1 lb.) grape leaves, drained
boiling water
1 cup minced onion
5¼ cups hot chicken stock, divided
2 tsp. salt, divided
1 cup uncooked rice
½ cup pine nuts
½ cup raisins
1 tsp. chopped fresh parsley
½ tsp. dill seeds

3 cloves garlic, minced
1 tsp. dried oregano
1 tsp. ground cumin
½ tsp. ground allspice
1 tsp. dried mint
⅓ cup fresh lemon juice
2 tbs. extra-virgin olive oil
1 tsp. salt
sliced lemon wedges for garnish

Wash grape leaves 3 times in cold water to remove excess brine. Soak leaves in boiling water for 1¼ hours, until pliable. In a skillet over medium heat, sauté onion for 1 minute to remove excess moisture. Add ¼ cup of the chicken stock and simmer for 5 minutes. Add 1 tsp. of the salt, rice, pine nuts, raisins, parsley, dill, garlic, oregano, cumin, allspice, mint and 1 cup of the chicken stock. Cover and simmer for 10 minutes. Stir in ½ of the lemon juice and cool.

Remove thick stem from each grape leaf. Place a layer of grape leaves in a heavy pot and arrange remaining leaves on a work surface, shiny-side down. Place between 1 tsp. and 1 tbs. filling, depending on size of leaves, at the base of each leaf. Fold sides of leaf in over filling and roll up tightly.

Place filled grape leaves in layers in pot. Pour remaining 4 cups chicken stock, remaining lemon juice and oil over rolls and sprinkle with remaining 1 tsp. salt. Place a heavy plate on top of rolls to prevent stuffed leaves from unrolling and cover pot with lid. Cook over low heat for 25 minutes, or until liquid is totally absorbed. Transfer rolls to a serving platter and cool. Garnish with lemon wedges.

BACON-STUFFED CHERRY TOMATOES

Make plenty of these extremely popular appetizers because they will go fast!

2 lb. bacon, finely diced
⅓ cup chopped green onions
½ cup mayonnaise
24 large cherry tomatoes, stems removed
lettuce leaves for garnish

In a skillet, cook bacon until browned and crisp. Transfer to paper towels to drain and cool. Crumble bacon and mix in a bowl with green onions and mayonnaise until well blended. Refrigerate until ready to use.

Cut a small a small piece from the bottom of each tomato (opposite the stem end). From stem end, scoop out tomato pulp with a melon baller or small spoon, being careful not to break through the bottom of the tomatoes. Place hollowed tomatoes hole-side down on paper towels for about 15 minutes to drain. Fill tomato cavities with bacon mixture and place stem-side up on a serving platter. Surround tomatoes with lettuce and refrigerate until ready to serve.

TUNA-STUFFED EGGS

Here's a new take on deviled eggs. For a colorful variation, add 2 tsp. finely chopped sun-dried tomatoes to the filling. Or, for a more traditional flavor, add 1 tbs. sweet pickle relish.

12 hard-cooked eggs, peeled
1 can (6½ oz.) water-packed tuna, drained
¼ cup (½ stick) butter, softened
2 tsp. Dijon mustard
1 tbs. mayonnaise or cream cheese
1 tsp. minced garlic

salt and pepper
1 pinch cayenne pepper
1 tbs. chopped fresh parsley
1 tbs. capers
finely chopped red bell pepper for garnish
24 small sprigs parsley for garnish

Slice eggs in half horizontally and place yolks in a small bowl. Cut a sliver from the bottom of each egg white half so that they won't wobble. Mash egg yolks finely with a fork. To bowl, add tuna, butter, mustard, mayonnaise, garlic, salt, pepper, cayenne, chopped parsley and capers and mix well. Taste and adjust seasonings. Generously spoon egg yolk mixture into egg white halves. Place on a serving platter and garnish each filled egg with a few pieces of red pepper and a small sprig of parsley.

MARBLED TEA EGGS

Here is a fancy version of deviled eggs. Using vegetables as natural dyes, hard-cooked eggs are steeped in colored water to create a beautiful marbleized pink, green or yellow effect. If desired, garnish each egg with a small piece of parsley and a tiny sliver of red bell pepper. For the beet juice, strain the juice from canned beets.

18 eggs
1 tbs. salt
3 pkg. (10 oz. each) frozen chopped
   spinach
1½ cups water
peels from 4 yellow onions
2½ cups water

2 cups beet juice
½ cup mayonnaise
3 oz. cream cheese
½ cup (1 stick) butter, softened
1 dash Worcestershire sauce
1 tsp. Dijon mustard
salt and white pepper

In a large saucepan, place eggs, 1 tbs. salt and enough cold water to cover eggs by 1 inch. Bring to a boil. Cover, reduce heat to low and cook for 20 minutes. Drain at once and chill in ice water for 5 minutes. Roll eggs gently on a work surface or between your hands until shells are cracked; do not peel.

In a saucepan, combine spinach and 1 1/2 cups water and bring to a boil. Reduce heat to low, cover and simmer for 30 minutes. Strain juice and cool to room temperature. Place 6 eggs in a small, deep bowl and cover with spinach juice. Steep overnight in the refrigerator.

In another saucepan, combine onion peels and 2 1/2 cups water and bring to a boil. Reduce heat to low and simmer for 20 minutes. Strain juice and cool to room temperature. Place 6 of the eggs in a small, deep bowl and cover with onion juice. Steep overnight in the refrigerator.

Place remaining 6 eggs in a small, deep bowl and cover with beet juice. Steep overnight in the refrigerator.

Remove eggs from juices and remove peels. Split eggs in half horizontally and remove yolks. Cut a sliver from the bottom of each egg white half so that they won't wobble. In a food processor workbowl or in a bowl with a mixer, process yolks with mayonnaise, cream cheese, butter, Worcestershire, mustard, salt and pepper until smooth; taste and adjust seasonings. Place mixture in a pastry bag with a decorative tip and pipe into egg halves. Place filled eggs on a serving platter.

CUCUMBER-HERB CANAPÉS

Makes about 36 pieces

For this delicate and refreshing appetizer, the cucumbers can be cut into shapes to follow a theme, such as hearts for Valentine's Day.

2 large cucumbers (I prefer English variety),
   peeled and cut into ¼-inch slices
1 clove garlic, minced
¼ cup chopped fresh parsley
2 green onions, chopped
8 oz. cream cheese, softened

1 dash Tabasco Sauce
1 tbs. dry white wine
salt to taste
white pepper to taste
finely minced red bell pepper or 36 small
   sprigs parsley for garnish

If desired, use a cookie cutter to cut cucumbers slices into shapes. In a food processor workbowl or blender container, process garlic, parsley and onions until finely minced. Add cream cheese, Tabasco, wine, salt and white pepper and process until well mixed. Taste and adjust seasonings. Transfer ingredients to a pastry bag with a decorative tip and pipe mixture onto cucumber slices. Place on a serving platter, garnish and refrigerate until ready to serve.

CUCUMBER-MINT COOLERS

For your next tea party, serve these light and refreshing cucumber tea sandwiches.

1 large cucumber, peeled and very thinly sliced
1½ tsp. salt
2½ tbs. chopped fresh mint
½ tsp. sugar
1 tsp. lemon juice
¾ cup (1½ sticks) butter, softened
16 slices white bread, crusts removed
pepper to taste
24 sprigs mint for garnish

Place cucumber slices in a colander, sprinkle with salt and set aside to drain for 30 minutes. Pat cucumbers dry on paper towels and set aside. In a food processor workbowl or blender container, process mint with sugar until finely minced. Add lemon juice and butter and process until smooth. Spread butter mixture on bread slices. Divide cucumbers among ½ of the buttered bread slices and sprinkle with pepper. Cover cucumbers with remaining bread slices, buttered-side down. Cut each sandwich into 3 long strips and serve garnished with mint.

BASIC TEA SANDWICHES

Here is a new twist on an old-fashioned tea party favorite. This recipe works best with a firm variety of pear, such as Bosc. A dense bread, such as potato or egg bread (challah), makes a firmer sandwich.

PEAR AND CUCUMBER TEA SANDWICHES

8 slices potato, egg or white bread, crusts removed
8 oz. cream cheese, softened
1 cucumber, peeled and thinly sliced
1 firm ripe pear, peeled if desired, cored and thinly sliced

Spread each bread slice generously with cream cheese. Cover ½ of the bread slices with sliced cucumber and pear, dividing evenly. Cover with remaining bread slices, cheese-side down. Cut each sandwich into 3 strips, place on a serving platter and refrigerate until ready to serve.

PEAR, CUCUMBER AND GORGONZOLA TEA SANDWICHES

Mix 1 to 2 oz. crumbled Gorgonzola cheese with cream cheese.

PEAR, CUCUMBER AND MINT TEA SANDWICHES

Mix 1 tbs. chopped fresh mint with cream cheese. If desired, add ½ to 1 tsp. sugar.

PEAR, CUCUMBER AND GOAT CHEESE TEA SANDWICHES

Replace cream cheese with soft goat cheese.

SMOKED CHEESE TEA SANDWICHES WITH CUCUMBER OR PEAR

Use either cucumber or pear and add a thin slice of smoked cheddar cheese. Add a small amount of paprika for color, if desired.

CUCUMBER AND SUN-DRIED TOMATO TEA SANDWICHES

Mix ¼ cup chopped sun-dried tomatoes with cream cheese. Omit pear.

PUMPKIN TEA SANDWICHES

Makes about 60 sandwiches

This sweet appetizer is ideal to serve during the fall season. Serve with either Orange Butter or Mango Spread (recipe to follow).

1 cup (2 sticks) butter, softened
2 tbs. molasses
3 cups sugar
6 large eggs
1 cup orange juice
1 tbs. grated fresh orange zest
1 can (30 oz.) pumpkin puree
5 cups flour

1 tsp. baking powder
1 tbs. baking soda
¼ tsp. salt
1½ tsp. cinnamon
½ tsp. ground cloves
1½ cups raisins or dried currants
Orange Butter or Mango Spread, follow

Heat oven to 350°. Line three 9 x 5-inch loaf pans with parchment or brown paper and butter the sides of pan. In a large bowl with a mixer, beat butter, molasses and sugar until light and fluffy. Beat in eggs until mixture is lemon-colored. Add orange juice, orange peel and pumpkin and mix well. In a separate bowl, mix flour, baking powder, baking soda, salt, cinnamon and cloves and add to pumpkin mixture, mixing well. Stir in raisins. Divide mixture evenly among pans and bake for about 1 hour, or until a knife inserted into the center comes out clean. Cool bread in pans for 10 minutes before transferring to racks to cool completely. Cut bread into 1/2-inch slices and cut slices in half. Spread each slice with Orange Butter or Mango Spread and place open-faced slices in a single layer on a serving platter. Serve at room temperature.

ORANGE BUTTER

½ cup (1 stick) unsalted butter, softened
¼ cup orange marmalade

In a food processor workbowl or in a bowl with an electric mixer, mix butter and marmalade until well blended.

MANGO SPREAD

8 oz. cream cheese, softened
½ cup mango chutney

Stir ingredients together until blended.

DATE BREAD WITH PINEAPPLE CREAM CHEESE

Makes 40 pieces

Make this bread ahead of time and freeze it. When thawed, cut into small rectangular shapes and spread with cream cheese mixture. Garnish the serving platter with edible flowers.

2 cups boiling water
1 lb. chopped pitted dates
2 tbs. butter
2 tsp. baking soda
2 cups sugar
3½ cups flour

2 tsp. vanilla extract
1 cup chopped walnuts
8 oz. cream cheese, softened
1 can (10½ oz.) crushed pineapple, drained
sugar to taste, optional

Heat oven to 325°. Line two 9 x 5-inch loaf pans with parchment or brown paper and grease well. In a bowl, mix water, dates and butter together; cool. Add baking soda, sugar, flour, vanilla and nuts to bowl, stirring until just mixed. Divide batter evenly among pans and bake for about 1 hour, or until a knife inserted into the center comes out clean. Cool bread in pans for 10 minutes before transferring to racks to cool completely.

Cut cooled bread into ½-inch slices and cut each slice in half. In a bowl, beat cream cheese with pineapple and sugar, if using. Spread each slice with cream cheese mixture and arrange on a serving platter.

SMOKED TURKEY ROLLS

Serve this fast, easy-to-fix appetizer with honey-mustard dressing for dipping.

1 lb. smoked turkey, sliced
½ lb. cotto salami, thinly sliced
8 oz. cream cheese, softened
½ red bell pepper, thinly sliced
½ yellow bell pepper, thinly sliced
½ green bell pepper, thinly sliced
lettuce leaves, for garnish

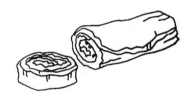

Place a slice of smoked turkey on a piece of plastic wrap. Cover with salami, spread with cream cheese and place 1 strip pepper of each color in center. Roll tightly and refrigerate. Repeat with remaining turkey, salami, cream cheese and peppers. To serve, cut each roll into ½-inch slices and serve on a bed of lettuce.

CHICKEN RELISH SWIRLS

Here's a good way to use leftover chicken. To make clean slices, make sure the rolls are well chilled before cutting.

8 oz. cooked boneless chicken
4 tsp. mango chutney
1 tbs. mayonnaise
1/4 cup chopped green bell pepper
4 green onions, chopped
4 gherkins, chopped

1/4–1/2 tsp. curry powder
salt and pepper to taste
6 slices white bread, crusts removed
1/2 cup (1 stick) butter, softened
about 1 cup stuffed green olives
chopped fresh cilantro for garnish

In a food processor workbowl, process chicken until finely minced. Add chutney, mayonnaise, pepper, green onion, pickles, curry powder, salt and pepper and process just until mixed. Taste and adjust seasonings.

With a rolling pin, flatten bread slices and spread with butter. Spread each buttered slice with chicken mixture and arrange a row of olives along the edge of each slice. Roll up bread tightly, jelly-roll style, and wrap securely with plastic wrap. Refrigerate for at least 2 hours. Cut each roll at an angle into 4 slices. Place slices in a single layer on a serving platter and garnish with cilantro.

SMOKED SALMON TREATS

These tasty appetizers are relatively quick to fix. If desired, you can substitute 1 can (7¼ oz.) salmon and 4 drops Liquid Smoke for the smoked salmon.

8 oz. cream cheese, softened
8 oz. smoked salmon, chopped
3 tbs. minced green onion
½ loaf sliced white or rye bread, crusts removed
½ cup (1 stick) butter, softened
paprika for garnish

In a bowl, mix cream cheese with salmon and green onion until well mixed. On a work surface, flatten bread with a rolling pin. Spread butter over half of the slices on one side. With a fluted round 2-inch cutter, cut 2 circles from each slice of bread. Spread salmon mixture on buttered bread shapes and place on a platter. Spread remaining bread slices with butter on both sides and cut into shapes with cutter. Cover each salmon-covered slice with buttered slices, lining up the edges. Press halves lightly together, sprinkle each buttered top with paprika and refrigerate until ready to serve.

SHRIMP SALAD PUFFS

Makes about 24 puffs

These little cream puffs are filled with a subtly flavored shrimp salad mixture. Be sure to beat the cream puff batter very well. The beating action develops the gluten in the flour, which helps the puffs to rise high. Don't fill the puffs until just before serving or they will get soggy.

½ cup (1 stick) butter
1 pinch salt
1 cup water
1 cup flour
4 eggs
3 oz. cream cheese, softened
1 jar (4 oz.) olive pimiento cheese spread
½ cup blue cheese salad dressing

½ cup mayonnaise
2 tbs. ketchup
¼ tsp. Worcestershire sauce
¼ tsp. prepared horseradish
1 tbs. lemon juice, or to taste
1 clove garlic, minced
1 can (6 oz.) shrimp

Heat oven to 400°. In a saucepan, bring butter, salt and water to a boil; remove from heat. Add flour to pan all at once and stir until dough comes together in a ball and leaves the sides of pan. Cool dough slightly. Add eggs to dough, one at a time, beating very vigorously after each egg is added, until a smooth batter is formed. Drop batter by teaspoonfuls onto a greased cookie sheet. Bake for 10 minutes, reduce oven heat to 350° and bake for 20 minutes. Remove puffs from oven and place on wire racks to cool.

Process cream cheese, pimiento cheese, dressing, mayonnaise, ketchup, Worcestershire, horseradish, lemon juice and garlic in a food processor workbowl or blender container until well mixed. Transfer to a bowl and stir in shrimp.

To serve, split cooled puffs in half, fill with shrimp mixture and place on a serving platter. If not serving immediately, store puffs at room temperature in an airtight container and refrigerate filling in a covered bowl. Assemble just before serving.

PASTA SHELLS FILLED WITH SHRIMP AND VEGETABLES

Stuffed pasta shells are a quick, substantial appetizer that can be made ahead of time. For a luncheon entree, serve several of these on each plate.

½ cup chopped water chestnuts
2 cups chopped celery
2 cups grated carrots
¼–½ cup chopped green onions
2 cups cooked baby shrimp
2 cups (8 oz.) shredded regular or low-fat
  sharp cheddar cheese

1 cup regular or low-fat mayonnaise
1 tbs. lemon juice, or to taste
1 tsp. sugar
1 lb. jumbo pasta shells, cooked, drained
  and cooled
lettuce leaves, for garnish

In a bowl, mix water chestnuts, celery, carrots, green onions, shrimp and cheddar cheese until well mixed. In a separate bowl, mix mayonnaise, lemon juice and sugar until blended; stir into shrimp mixture. Fill pasta shells with shrimp mixture and refrigerate until ready to serve. Line a serving platter with lettuce leaves and arrange stuffed shells on top.

STRAWBERRIES STUFFED WITH ORANGE CREAM CHEESE

Refresh your guests with this sweet appetizer, or use this recipe as a light dessert. If desired, surround the fruit with attractive greenery, such as fresh mint, watercress or well-cleaned greens from the garden. Use Grand Marnier, curaçao or Triple Sec for the liqueur.

1 pt. strawberries
8 oz. cream cheese, softened
¼ cup confectioner's sugar, or to taste
2 tbs. orange-flavored liqueur, or to taste

Remove stems from berries to create a flat surface so that berries stand with their points facing up. With a small knife, cut an X through the pointed end of each berry ¼ of the way down. Place berries on their bases on a serving dish. In a bowl with a mixer or in a food processor workbowl, process cream cheese with sugar and liqueur until well blended. Place mixture into a pastry bag with a star tip. Pipe cream cheese mixture into the center of each berry. Serve immediately.

FRUIT KABOBS

Fruit makes a refreshing appetizer that is ideal to serve during the summer months. Kids especially love this one.

3 bananas, peeled
3 apples
2 tbs. lemon juice mixed with 1 cup cold water
3 kiwi fruits, peeled and cut into chunks

2 oranges, peeled and sectioned
1 cantaloupe, honeydew, watermelon or other melon, rind removed and cut into cubes
1 cup fresh or canned pineapple chunks

DIPPING SAUCES
nonfat sour cream mixed with orange juice and honey to taste, optional
low-fat or nonfat flavored yogurt, optional
plain yogurt flavored with extracts to taste, optional
granola for coating, optional

Cut bananas into chunks. Core apples, peel if desired and cut into large chunks. Dip bananas and apples in lemon juice mixture to prevent darkening. Thread bananas, apples, kiwi, oranges, melon and pineapple on wooden skewers, alternating types. Refrigerate until ready to serve. Serve with your choice of dipping sauces and granola, if desired.

CREAMY STUFFED DATES

Garnish this quick and easy recipe with twisted orange slices and a few mint sprigs.

40 whole pitted dates
8 oz. regular, low-fat or nonfat cream cheese, softened
⅓ cup orange flavored liqueur
sugar to taste, optional
2 tbs, grated fresh orange zest

Cut dates in half lengthwise and place cut-side up on a serving platter. In a bowl, mix cream cheese with orange liqueur and sugar. Place cream cheese mixture in a pastry bag with a decorative tip and pipe into date halves. Sprinkle with grated orange zest.

HOT FINGER FOODS

HOT BERRIED CHEESE

Use this technique with any double or triple crème soft cheese. Changing the flavor of breadcrumbs by altering the spices will give you endless variations. In the place of pepper try using Italian spice mix, garlic powder, or even chopped nuts. I like to serve the fried cheese on a bed of red cabbage or radicchio.

1 lb. Tourrée de L'Aubier, Brie or other double/triple cream cheese
1 cup plain dry breadcrumbs
½ tsp. black pepper (or spice of choice)
2 eggs, beaten
peanut or vegetable oil for frying
½ cup gooseberry, lingonberry, blueberry or apricot jam

Cut cheese into eight 2-oz. pieces and remove rind. Refrigerate cheese for at least 1 hour. Mix breadcrumbs with pepper in a bowl. Beat eggs in a separate bowl. Dip each cheese piece in eggs, then coat with seasoned crumbs. Place on a plate and refrigerate for 15 minutes before frying. Heat oil to 350° in a deep-fat fryer or saucepan. Fry cheese until coating turns golden brown. Spoon a dollop of jam on top and serve immediately with slices of French bread.

COCONUT PRAWNS

This recipe can serve as an appetizer or main dish. It goes well with a slightly sweet bottled sauce like apricot sauce, peanut sauce, pineapple chutney or a light curry dip.

peanut or vegetable oil for frying
24 large (20 count) prawns
½ cup cornstarch
⅓ tsp. salt
⅓ tsp. white pepper

⅓ tsp. cayenne pepper
4–5 egg whites
3 cups shredded sweetened coconut
salt, optional

Heat oil in a deep-fat fryer or deep saucepan to 350°. Peel, devein and butterfly prawns then dry with paper towels. Place cornstarch, salt, pepper and cayenne in a bowl and stir to combine. In a separate bowl, whisk the egg whites until foamy. Place shredded coconut in a third bowl. Dredge prawns in cornstarch mixture, shaking off any excess. Dip in egg whites and then press into shredded coconut. Fry coated prawns in small batches for about 3 minutes. Drain on paper towels and gently sprinkle with a little salt (the salt tends to reduce some of the greasiness from deep fat frying). Serve immediately with dipping sauce of choice.

SESAME SALMON BITES

Serve this quick appetizer with Orange Mayonnaise Dip, *page 39. I like to use regular and black sesame seeds for a beautiful presentation. A firm-fleshed fish like tuna can be substituted for the salmon.*

1½ lbs. salmon filet
3 tbs. extra-virgin olive oil
salt and pepper to taste
3 tbs. sesame seeds
3 tbs. black sesame seeds

Heat oven to 400°. Remove skin from filet and cut into ½-inch cubes. Place fish cubes in a bowl along with olive oil, salt and pepper and gently toss to coat the cubes. In a separate bowl, mix sesame seeds together. Line a cookie sheet with foil, dip one end of fish cubes in the sesame mixture and place (sesame side up) on the cookie sheet. Bake, uncovered, for 5 to 6 minutes. Skewer cubes with toothpicks. Serve immediately.

GOAT CHEESE-STUFFED PRAWNS

One of my favorite finds is using prosciutto in place of bacon. It adds more flavor and produces less greasy results. Generally, I allow three prawns per person as an appetizer.

4 oz. soft goat cheese
1½ tbs. chopped fresh parsley
1 tbs. minced garlic
2 tsp. finely chopped fresh rosemary
2 tsp. chopped fresh oregano
salt and pepper to taste
12 large prawns, peeled and tails left on
12 slices prosciutto
3 tbs. olive oil

In a small bowl, combine goat cheese, parsley, garlic, rosemary, oregano, salt and pepper. Taste and adjust seasonings. Butterfly the prawns and stuff each with 2 to 3 tsp. of filling. Sprinkle prawns with salt and pepper then wrap each prawn tightly with one piece of prosciutto. Heat olive oil on medium-high in a sauté pan and sear for 2 to 3 minutes per side, or until prawns turn pink. Serve immediately.

WARM CHEESE WAFERS

This is a great recipe to keep frozen and ready to bake for drop-in guests.

½ cup (1 stick) butter, cut into pieces
½ lb. Brie cheese, rind removed and cubed, or ½ lb. sharp cheddar cheese, shredded
1 cup flour
¼ tsp. seasoned salt
½ tsp. Tabasco Sauce
¼ cup sesame seeds

In a food processor workbowl or in a bowl with a mixer, process butter and cheese until well blended. Add flour, seasoned salt and Tabasco and mix until a smooth dough forms. Divide dough into 4 equal pieces and shape each piece into a 1-inch-diameter log. Wrap logs with waxed paper and refrigerate or freeze until ready to serve.

Heat oven to 400°. Cut each log into ¼-inch slices. Place slices 1 inch apart on ungreased cookie sheets and sprinkle with sesame seeds. Bake for 8 to 10 minutes or until edges are golden brown. Cool slightly and serve immediately.

FRIED CHEESE SQUARES

Makes about 12 squares

This favorite Greek appetizer is typically served with retsina wine and crusty bread. Look for the cheeses in a Greek deli or specialty store.

½ lb. Kefalotiri, kasseri, Asiago or Romano cheese
¼ cup olive oil
¼ cup (½ stick) butter
3 large eggs, beaten with a little water
1 cup flour

2 tbs. brandy
2 tbs. lemon juice
¼ tsp. dried oregano
2 tbs. chopped fresh parsley
lemon wedges, for garnish

Heat oven to 400°. Place an ovenproof dish in oven to heat. Cut cheese into twelve ¼-inch-thick squares or triangles. In a deep skillet, heat oil and butter over medium heat. Dip cheese squares in beaten eggs and dredge in flour. Carefully place coated cheese in skillet and fry until golden brown on both sides. Remove heated dish from oven and place cheese on it.

In a small saucepan, heat brandy until just below the boiling point and immediately pour over cheese. Carefully tilt dish and ignite hot brandy with a match. When flames have died down, sprinkle with lemon juice, oregano and parsley. Serve immediately, garnished with lemon wedges.

FRENCH CAVIAR POTATOES

For this simple and sophisticated presentation, arrange potatoes on a bed of shredded lettuce or fresh parsley. If desired, use 2 colors of caviar for eye appeal and variety.

60 tiny new potatoes, unpeeled, cooked until tender
oil for deep frying
8 oz. sour cream
1 jar (2 oz.) caviar, rinsed and drained

Heat oven to 200°. Slice a small piece from the bottom of each potato so that they won't wobble. With a melon baller or small spoon, scoop out the centers of potatoes; reserve centers for another use or discard. Heat oil in a deep fryer or deep pan to 375°. Carefully drop prepared potatoes into hot oil and fry until crisp. Remove potatoes with a strainer and drain on paper towels; keep warm on a cookie sheet in oven until ready to serve. Just before serving, fill warm potatoes with sour cream and top with a small amount of caviar. Serve immediately.

MINIATURE FRENCH QUICHES

These are best served slightly warm, but they can also be served at room temperature. For ease, assemble this recipe ahead of time and freeze. Thaw quiches for 2 to 3 hours in the refrigerator before baking.

2 cups flour
1 pinch salt
³/₄ cup (1½ sticks) cold butter, cut into pieces
⅓ cup cold water
8 slices bacon, finely diced
1 medium onion, diced
4 eggs, beaten

1 cup milk
1 cup heavy cream
¼ tsp. nutmeg
½ tsp. salt
¼ tsp. pepper
¼ cup chopped green chiles, optional
¼ cup (1 oz.) shredded Swiss cheese
¼ cup (1 oz.) shredded cheddar cheese

In a food processor workbowl, process flour, salt and butter just until crumbly. Add water and process until dough just holds together; take care not to overmix. Remove dough, wrap with plastic wrap and refrigerate for 30 minutes. On a lightly floured work surface, roll dough to ⅛-inch thick. With a 2½-inch round fluted cutter, cut dough into 32 rounds. Line miniature muffin tins with pastry dough and refrigerate until ready to fill.

Heat oven to 450°. In a skillet, fry bacon pieces over medium-high heat until crisp and drain on paper towels. Add onion to skillet with bacon fat and sauté over medium heat until wilted. In a bowl, mix eggs, milk, cream, nutmeg, salt and pepper until blended. Distribute bacon, onion, chiles and cheeses evenly among pastry shells. Pour egg mixture into pastry shells, dividing evenly. Bake for 10 minutes. Reduce oven heat to 350° and bake for about 8 minutes, until eggs are set.

RED ONION FOCACCIA

You'll love the delicious cooked onion topping on this well-loved Italian flatbread. Make it on a pizza pan and cut it into small squares or wedges. For ease, you can make the dough with a bread machine, using the dough cycle.

2 tsp. active dry yeast
1 pinch sugar
1 cup warm water
2½ cups flour
½ tsp. salt
⅓ cup plus 1 tbs. olive oil, divided
1¾ lb. red onions, thinly sliced
1 tsp. anchovy paste
1 tbs. white vinegar
olive oil for brushing
salt and pepper to taste

In a bowl, dissolve yeast and sugar in warm water. Add about 1 cup of the flour and beat vigorously for 1 minute. Let mixture rise in a warm, draft-free place until doubled in bulk, about 30 minutes. Punch mixture down and add salt, 1 tbs. of the oil and remaining flour, a little at a time, until dough comes together in a ball and is not too sticky. On a floured work surface, knead dough well for about 10 minutes. Let dough rest for 15 minutes.

In a skillet over low heat, cook onions in remaining ⅓ cup olive oil until softened. Dissolve anchovy paste in vinegar and add to skillet with onions. Cook over medium heat until onions are soft and liquid has evaporated, about 5 minutes. Set aside to cool.

Punch down dough and shape to fit a 12-inch pizza pan. Let rise in a warm, draft-free place for 30 minutes. Heat oven to 400°. Brush dough lightly with olive oil and sprinkle with salt and pepper. Taste onions, adjusting seasonings if necessary, and spread gently on dough within ½-inch of edge. Bake in oven for 30 to 35 minutes until lightly browned. To serve, cut into small squares with a pizza cutter or large knife.

QUESADILLAS

Serve this cheesy Mexican-style delight with Guacamole, *page 29, and sour cream for dipping. Be sure to provide lots of napkins!*

1 cup (4 oz.) shredded sharp cheddar cheese
1 cup (4 oz.) shredded Monterey Jack cheese
vegetable oil for frying
twelve 8-inch flour tortillas
4 green onions, chopped
1 can (4 oz.) diced green chiles, drained

Heat oven to 200°. Mix cheeses together. In a skillet over medium heat, add enough oil to coat bottom of pan and heat. Place 1 tortilla in pan. Sprinkle with ⅙ each of the cheese, green onions and diced chiles. Cover with another tortilla. When tortilla is golden brown on the bottom, flip quesadilla over with a spatula. Cook until opposite side is golden brown and cheese is melted. Transfer quesadilla to a paper towel-lined cookie sheet and keep warm in oven. Repeat cooking process with remaining ingredients, adding a layer of paper towels between each layer of quesadillas. To serve, cut each quesadilla into 6 wedges and serve immediately.

MUSHROOM PHYLLO TARTS

Makes 24 tarts

Phyllo dough-lined muffin tins feature a wonderful mushroom and onion filling. Try this recipe with different varieties of mushrooms for a delightful change. Always keep phyllo dough under a damp towel while working to keep it from drying out.

4 sheets phyllo dough, thawed if frozen
6 tbs. *Clarified Butter*, page 131
1 lb. white or brown mushrooms, chopped
½ cup chopped onion

¼ cup chopped fresh parsley
½ cup dry white wine
1 dash Tabasco Sauce
1 cup (4 oz.) shredded Monterey Jack cheese

Heat oven to 400°. Place 1 sheet of the phyllo on a work surface and brush with Clarified Butter. Cover with another phyllo sheet and brush again with butter. Repeat layering and brushing with remaining phyllo. Cut phyllo stack into 24 squares and place each square in a miniature muffin cup. In a skillet over medium-high heat, sauté mushrooms with onion, parsley, wine and Tabasco until liquid is almost evaporated; cool. Fill phyllo cups with mushroom mixture and top with cheese, dividing evenly. Bake for 15 to 18 minutes, until phyllo is golden brown and filling is hot. Keep warm in a chafing dish, or in a dish set on an electric warming tray.

PESTO MUSHROOMS

These whip together in minutes. For another variation, use chive-flavored cream cheese and crumbled bacon instead of pesto.

2 tbs. butter
1 clove garlic, minced
16 large white or brown mushrooms
salt and pepper to taste
4 oz. cream cheese, softened
1/3 cup purchased pesto

In a small saucepan, melt butter over medium heat and sauté garlic until soft, but not browned. Set aside. Cut stems from mushrooms at base of caps. Reserve mushroom stems for another use or discard. Brush mushroom caps with garlic butter mixture and place stem-side up in an ovenproof dish. Sprinkle caps with salt and pepper. Mix cream cheese with pesto until blended and mound mixture in the center of each cap, dividing evenly. Refrigerate for several hours or overnight.

When ready to serve, heat oven to 400°. Bake mushrooms for 5 to 6 minutes or until filling is soft and mushrooms are warm. Serve hot in a chafing dish, or in a baking dish set on an electric warming tray.

PATÉ MUSHROOMS

Paté is available in a variety of flavors and textures in many grocery stores and specialty food stores. Experiment with your favorite type of paté for this simple, fast recipe.

60 medium white or brown mushrooms
¼ lb. paté, mashed with a fork
finely chopped fresh parsley for garnish

Heat broiler. Cut stems from mushrooms at base of caps. Reserve mushroom stems for another use or discard. Place mushrooms stem-side up on a cookie sheet and fill each cap with a small mound of paté. Broil for 2 to 3 minutes, until piping hot. Garnish with parsley. Serve hot in a chafing dish, or in a baking dish set on an electric warming tray.

SPINACH-STUFFED MUSHROOMS

Squeeze the spinach very dry. Otherwise, the filling leaches too much liquid and the appetizer is too messy to handle.

2 tbs. butter
¼ cup minced onion
1 cup chopped frozen spinach, thawed and squeezed very dry
½ cup low-fat ricotta cheese
¼ cup (1 oz.) grated Parmesan cheese
salt and pepper to taste
grated nutmeg to taste
1 lb. medium white or brown mushrooms

Heat oven to 350°. In a skillet, heat butter over medium heat and sauté onion until limp. Remove from heat. Add spinach, ricotta cheese, Parmesan cheese, salt, pepper and nutmeg; taste and adjust seasonings. Cut stems from mushrooms at base of caps. Reserve mushroom stems for another use or discard. Place mushrooms stem-side up on a cookie sheet and fill each cap with a small mound of filling. Bake for about 20 minutes. Serve hot in a chafing dish, or in a baking dish set on an electric warming tray.

HAWAIIAN-STYLE STUFFED MUSHROOMS

Makes 16 mushrooms

This rich, creamy appetizer is elegant enough to use as a starter for a fancy meal. Serve it with crusty rolls. To set the ambiance, use exotic Hawaiian flowers as a centerpiece for the table or buffet.

¼ cup (½ stick) butter
3 large sweet onions, thinly sliced
16 extra-large white or brown mushrooms
4 oz. fresh crabmeat
1 green onion, finely chopped

3 oz. cream cheese
salt and pepper to taste
1 cup (4 oz.) shredded Monterey Jack
 cheese

Heat oven to 350°. In a skillet, melt butter over medium-high heat and sauté onions until golden brown. Transfer onions to a casserole, or divide among 8 individual ramekins. Cut stems from mushrooms at base of caps. Reserve mushroom stems for another use or discard. Place mushrooms cap-side up in casserole or ramekins on top of onions. Mix together crabmeat, green onion, cream cheese, salt and pepper. Fill each mushroom cap with a small mound of crabmeat mixture. Bake for 5 to 8 minutes or until mushrooms are softened. Sprinkle with Monterey Jack and continue to bake until cheese melts. Serve hot in a chafing dish, or in a baking dish set on an electric warming tray.

CRAB-STUFFED MUSHROOMS

This chic appetizer is delicately flavored and rich. As a starter for a meal, limit the quantity to 2 stuffed mushrooms per person.

8 oz. cream cheese, softened
½ lb. crabmeat
1½ cups fine seasoned breadcrumbs
1 clove garlic, finely minced
16 extra-large white or brown mushrooms
2 tbs. grated Parmesan cheese
paprika for garnish

Heat broiler. In a bowl with a mixer, beat cream cheese until soft. Gently stir in crabmeat, breadcrumbs and garlic. Cut stems from mushrooms at base of caps. Reserve mushroom stems for another use or discard. Place mushrooms stem-side up on a cookie sheet and fill each mushroom cap with a small mound of crabmeat mixture. Sprinkle with Parmesan and paprika. Broil until piping hot, about 5 minutes. Serve hot in a chafing dish, or in a baking dish set on an electric warming tray.

CHEESY CRAB TOAST

This recipe is very simple, but it tastes complicated. In a pinch, imitation crabmeat can be substituted for crabmeat.

4 French rolls
½ cup (1 stick) butter, melted
6–8 tsp. Dijon mustard
12 oz. crabmeat
2 cups (8 oz.) shredded sharp cheddar cheese
2 tbs. minced fresh parsley
paprika, for garnish

Heat broiler. Cut rolls in half lengthwise and brush with melted butter. Place rolls on a cookie sheet buttered-side up and toast under broiler until golden brown. Remove rolls from oven and spread each half with mustard. Evenly distribute crabmeat among roll halves and sprinkle with cheese. Broil until cheese melts. Remove from oven and sprinkle with parsley and paprika. Cut rolls into 1-inch diagonal slices. Serve hot in a chafing dish, or in a baking dish set on an electric warming tray.

ASIAN SHRIMP TOAST

This popular appetizer should be fried just before the guests arrive. Or, provide a fondue pot filled with hot oil and let the guests to cook their own treats.

8 slices white bread, square loaf, crusts
   removed
1 lb. shrimp, peeled and deveined
½ cups finely minced onion
½ tsp. minced fresh ginger

1 tsp. salt
2 tsp. cornstarch
1 egg
sesame seeds for coating, optional
oil for deep frying

Cut each bread slice into 4 triangles and set aside to dry for 1 to 2 hours. Heat oven to 200°. Chop shrimp finely and place in a bowl. Add onion, ginger, salt, cornstarch and egg and mix into a smooth paste. Spread shrimp paste on bread triangles. If desired, dip bread triangles in sesame seeds. In a deep saucepan, wok or fondue pot, heat oil to 350°. Fry bread triangles until both sides are golden brown. Drain on paper towels. Serve hot in a chafing dish, or in a baking dish set on an electric warming tray.

MARINATED GRILLED SHRIMP

This very simple, tasteful appetizer wows your guests. If a grill is not available, the prawns can be quickly sautéed in the marinade mixture. Provide a small dish for the guests to place the shrimp tails after eating.

1 lb. large shrimp (18–24 per lb.)
1 cup olive oil
2 cloves garlic, minced
1 tsp. salt
½ tsp. chili powder
1 tbs. chopped fresh parsley

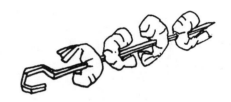

Peel shrimp, leaving tails intact. Mix oil, garlic, salt, chili powder and parsley together and pour over shrimp in a baking dish. Refrigerate for 1 hour. Prepare a medium-hot grill. Grill shrimp, basting with marinade, for about 3 minutes on each side, until shrimp turn pink; take care not to overcook. Serve hot in a chafing dish, or in a baking dish set on an electric warming tray.

BAKED CLAMS

For a dramatic presentation, arrange the clams on the half-shell on an ovenproof serving platter that is covered with rock salt. Provide a small dish for the discarded shells.

40 clams, well scrubbed
1/4 cup water
rock salt, optional
1/2 cup finely chopped fresh Italian parsley
4 cloves garlic, minced

1/2 cup dried breadcrumbs
1/4 cup olive oil or chicken stock
1/2 tsp. dried oregano
salt and pepper to taste

Place clams in a saucepan with water. Bring water to a boil over medium-high heat, cover pan tightly and steam just until clam shells open, about 2 minutes. Drain and discard any unopened shells. Snap off each top shell from clams and discard.

Heat broiler. Cover an ovenproof serving platter with a layer of rock salt, if desired, and arrange clam shells decoratively on platter. In a small bowl, mix parsley, garlic, breadcrumbs, oil, oregano, salt and pepper together, taste and adjust seasonings. Place a small amount of parsley mixture over each clam and broil until heated through and browned. Serve immediately.

TERIYAKI CHICKEN WINGS

These will disappear fast when serving a crowd, so be sure to make plenty. Keep them warm in a chafing dish and provide lots of napkins.

2 lb. chicken wings
1 small onion, chopped
½ cup soy sauce
½ cup brown sugar, firmly packed
1 tsp. minced fresh ginger
2 cloves garlic, minced
2 tbs. dry sherry
sesame seeds for garnish, optional

With a knife, separate chicken wings at the joints and discard tips. Place wing pieces in a baking dish. In a food processor workbowl or blender container, process onion, soy sauce, brown sugar, ginger, garlic and sherry until blended. Pour mixture over chicken and marinate in the refrigerator for at least 1 hour. Heat oven to 350°. Bake for 1 hour and sprinkle with sesame seeds, if using. Serve hot in a chafing dish, or in a baking dish set on an electric warming tray.

BARBECUED CHICKEN WINGS

This is a great recipe for traveling, because you can simply unplug the slow cooker and transport it to the party. To help your host, consider bringing an extension cord so the slow cooker can be easily placed. Remember to provide lots of napkins.

4 lb. chicken wings
2 large onions, chopped
2 cans (6 oz. each) tomato paste
2 large cloves garlic, minced
¼ cup Worcestershire sauce
¼ cup cider vinegar

½ cup brown sugar, packed
½ cup sweet pickle relish
½ cup red or white wine
2 tsp. salt
2 tsp. dry mustard

With a knife, separate chicken wings at the joints and discard tips. Place wing pieces in a large crockery pot or other slow cooker. Add remaining ingredients to pot and stir well. Set crockery pot on low and cook for 5 to 6 hours. Serve directly from crockery pot, in a chafing dish, or in a baking dish set on an electric warming tray.

HONEY CHICKEN WINGS

Chicken wings are fashionable fare for casual get-togethers. Make plenty of these — and don't forget the napkins.

3 lb. chicken wings
salt and pepper
1 cup honey
3 tbs. ketchup
½ cup soy sauce
2 tbs. vegetable oil
1 clove garlic, minced
sesame seeds for garnish, optional

Heat oven to 350°. With a knife, separate chicken wings at the joints and discard tips. Place wing pieces in a shallow baking dish and sprinkle with salt and pepper. In a small bowl, mix together honey, ketchup, soy sauce, oil and garlic and pour mixture over chicken. Bake for 50 minutes. Sprinkle with sesame seeds, if using. Serve hot in a chafing dish, or in a baking dish set on an electric warming tray.

TERIYAKI CHICKEN SKEWERS

Make this great recipe ahead of time — it takes just minutes to broil when the guests arrive.

3½ lb. boneless chicken breasts
¼ cup soy sauce
1 tbs. molasses
1½ cups dry white wine
1 cup water
2 tsp. salt
2 tsp. pepper
2 tsp. minced garlic
1 medium onion, minced
shredded lettuce, for garnish
Brandied Mayonnaise, follows, optional

Cut chicken breasts into thin strips, thread onto wooden skewers and place in a shallow pan. In a bowl, combine soy sauce, molasses, wine, water, salt, pepper, garlic and onion and pour over chicken strips. Cover pan and refrigerate overnight.

Heat broiler. Broil chicken pieces for about 3 minutes on each side, until cooked through. Serve on a bed of shredded lettuce alone or with a bowl of *Brandied Mayonnaise*.

BRANDIED MAYONNAISE

This makes a delightful change from the ordinary dipping sauce.

3/4 cup mayonnaise
1 tbs. brandy
3 tbs. ketchup
1 tbs. Worcestershire sauce
1 tbs. honey
1 tbs. lemon juice
salt and pepper

Blend all ingredients, taste and adjust seasonings. Cover and refrigerate until ready to serve.

SESAME-WALNUT CHICKEN STRIPS

Makes about 40 pieces

Using ground roasted Szechwan peppercorns creates a unique, fragrant taste sensation. Look for roasted Szechwan pepper in the international section of the supermarket or in an Asian market. If desired, serve these with homemade Sweet and Sour Sauce, *following.*

8 boneless, skinless chicken breast halves
2 cups walnuts
2 cups sesame seeds
oil for deep frying

salt to taste
ground roasted Szechwan pepper or black
  pepper to taste
Sweet and Sour Sauce, follows, optional

Heat oven to 200°. Cut each chicken breast half into 5 long strips. In a food processor workbowl or blender container, process walnuts with sesame seeds until finely ground and place in a shallow dish. In a deep pot, wok or fondue pot, heat oil to 350°. Dip chicken pieces into nut mixture and drop into hot oil. Fry for several minutes, turning once, until golden brown and cooked through. Remove chicken from oil, drain on paper towels and sprinkle with salt and pepper. Keep warm in oven until ready to serve. Cut strips into small diagonal pieces. Serve hot in a chafing dish, or in a baking dish set on an electric warming tray. Serve *Sweet and Sour Sauce*, if using, in a bowl on the side.

SWEET AND SOUR SAUCE

Here's an easy, tasty version of sweet and sour sauce.

3/4 cup pineapple juice
1/2 tbs. cornstarch
1/2 cup brown sugar, firmly packed
1 tsp. salt
1/2 cup cider vinegar
1/4 cup ketchup
1 cup crushed pineapple, drained
few drops red food coloring, optional

In a saucepan, mix pineapple juice with cornstarch. Add remaining ingredients and bring to a boil over medium-high heat, stirring constantly, until mixture thickens. Remove from heat. Serve warm or at room temperature.

SWEET AND SOUR MEATBALLS

You can make these into a meal for 4 to 6 people by serving them over rice.

½ cup fresh breadcrumbs
½ cup milk
1 lb. lean ground beef
¼ cup chopped onion
2 tsp. salt, divided
¼ tsp. pepper
2 eggs, beaten
½ cup flour

2 tbs. butter
1¼ cups cold water
1 tbs. cornstarch
¼ cup sugar
¼ cup vinegar
1 tbs. soy sauce
⅓ cup sliced green and/or red bell peppers

In a bowl, combine breadcrumbs and milk and let stand for 5 minutes. Add beef, onion, 1½ tsp. of the salt and pepper and blend well. Shape mixture into 32 balls. Dip balls in beaten eggs and roll in flour. In a large skillet, heat butter over medium-high heat. Add meatballs to skillet and brown on all sides. In a saucepan, combine water and cornstarch and stir until dissolved. Add sugar, vinegar, soy sauce and ½ tsp. salt. Add browned meatballs and cook over medium heat until mixture thickens. Add peppers, cover and simmer for 10 minutes. Serve hot in a chafing dish, or in a baking dish set on an electric warming tray. Provide toothpicks for serving.

PORK AND PINEAPPLE SKEWERS

Offer a bowl of plum sauce for dipping. It's a perfect partner for pork, but it also works well with beef or chicken. If time is limited, look for prepared plum sauce in the international section of the grocery store. Soak bamboo skewers in water for about 30 minutes before using so they won't burn while grilling.

6 cloves garlic, minced
1 tbs. ground coriander
1 tbs. turmeric
1 tbs. brown sugar
1 tbs. ground cumin

1 tsp. white pepper
1 tsp. salt
½ cup coconut milk
2 lb. pork tenderloin, thinly sliced
fresh pineapple, cut into ½-inch wedges

In a shallow dish, mix garlic, coriander, turmeric, brown sugar, cumin, white pepper, salt and coconut milk until blended. Add pork slices. Cover dish and refrigerate for several hours or overnight. Heat broiler or grill to high. Thread pork lengthwise onto soaked wooden skewers and thread a pineapple wedge at the end of each skewer. Grill or broil until cooked through, about 3 minutes per side. Serve hot in a chafing dish, or in a baking dish set on an electric warming tray.

HOISIN SPARERIBS

If you have trouble finding some of these ingredients, look in the international section of the supermarket or in an Asian market. Ask your butcher to cut the ribs crosswise into 1½-inch strips.

3 lb. pork spareribs, cut into 1½-inch strips
2 cloves garlic, minced
½ tsp. minced fresh ginger
3 tbs. hoisin sauce
2 tbs. sugar

¼ cup soy sauce
¼ cup dry sherry
¼ tsp. Chinese five-spice powder
½ cup water

Place ribs in a foil-lined shallow baking pan. Mix garlic, ginger, hoisin sauce, sugar, soy sauce, sherry and five-spice powder together, except water, and pour over ribs. Marinate for 1 hour in the refrigerator.

Heat oven to 300°. Add water to pan and cover with foil. Bake ribs for 2½ to 3 hours. Serve hot in a chafing dish, or in a baking dish set on an electric warming tray.

SWEET AND SOUR PUPUS

Makes about 48 pieces

Pupu is the Hawaiian word for appetizer. This favorite can be made ahead of time and baked just before the guests arrive. Scallops or cooked chicken livers can be substituted for the water chestnuts.

1 lb. bacon, cut into thirds
2 cans (4 oz. each) whole water chestnuts
¾ cup unsweetened pineapple juice
1½ tbs. cornstarch
½ cup brown sugar, firmly packed
½ cup cider vinegar

1 tsp. salt
4 tsp. ketchup
1 cup crushed unsweetened pineapple, drained
few drops red food coloring, optional

Heat oven to 350°. In a large pot of boiling water, cook bacon pieces for about 5 minutes; drain and cool. Wrap 1 piece of bacon around each water chestnut, secure with a toothpick and place in an ovenproof dish. In a saucepan, mix pineapple juice with cornstarch and bring to a boil. Add remaining ingredients and cook, stirring, until mixture is slightly thickened. Pour sauce over bacon-wrapped water chestnuts. Bake for 30 minutes until heated through. Serve hot in a chafing dish, or in a baking dish set on an electric warming tray.

WRAPPED DELICACIES

ASIAN FISH WRAPS

Using any firm fish and changing the vegetables can vary this healthy, low-carbohydrate appetizer. For a vegetarian version, use portobello mushrooms in the place of the fish. Bean sprouts can be substituted for the green onions.

10 oz. salmon filet, or any firm-fleshed fish	3–4 stalks green onions, shredded
salt and pepper	½ cup water
1 tsp. minced garlic	⅓ cup soy sauce
1 tsp. lime or lemon juice	⅓ cup rice wine vinegar
16 leaves Swiss chard or kale	sprinkling of sugar, optional

Sprinkle salmon with salt, pepper, garlic and lime juice. Cut filet into 12–16 pieces, about 3 inches long. Place seasoned fish on raw Swiss chard leaves and add several strands of green onions. Fold in the sides and roll into a bundle. Pour ½ cup water in skillet and bring to a boil. Add wraps, reduce heat to medium, cover and cook for 5 minutes. Uncover and cook for an additional 3 minutes more or until liquid evaporates. Serve with dipping sauce.

FOR SAUCE

In a bowl, combine soy sauce and rice wine vinegar. Taste and determine if you wish to add sugar for a slight sweet and sour taste.

THREE-CHEESE PHYLLO WITH WALNUTS

Wine tasting? Choose this delicate appetizer for a perfect accompaniment. While working with phyllo, keep it covered with a slightly damp cloth.

2 tbs. butter
1 clove garlic, minced
1 onion, finely chopped
½ cup crumbled Gorgonzola cheese
2 cups ricotta cheese
½ cup (2 oz.) grated Parmesan cheese

1 tbs. dried basil
1 tsp. ground fennel seeds
1 tsp. grated nutmeg
1 cup chopped toasted walnuts
1 pkg. (1 lb.) phyllo dough, thawed if frozen
Clarified Butter, page 131

Heat oven to 375°. In a skillet, melt butter over medium heat and sauté garlic and onion until tender. Remove skillet from heat and add cheeses, basil, fennel seeds, nutmeg and walnuts. Place 1 sheet of the phyllo on a work surface and brush with Clarified Butter. Cut phyllo lengthwise into 3 strips, fold each strip in half lengthwise and brush again with butter. Place a spoonful of cheese mixture in the top corner of each strip and fold like a flag into a triangular bundle. Brush outside of triangles with butter and place on a rimmed cookie sheet. Repeat with remaining ingredients. Bake triangles for 15 to 20 minutes or until golden brown. Serve warm.

MIDDLE EASTERN VEGETABLE PACKETS

Makes 24 pieces

This vegetarian appetizer is surrounded by flaky pastry. It can be made ahead of time and kept frozen until ready to bake; thaw before baking. Keep phyllo covered with a slightly damp cloth while working to prevent it from drying out.

2 tbs. butter
½ medium onion, diced
⅓ lb. white or brown mushrooms, diced
1 tbs. chopped fresh cilantro
1 tbs. chopped fresh parsley
1 tsp. ground cumin

½ tsp. salt
¼ tsp. pepper
16 sheets phyllo dough (about ½ pkg.),
  thawed if frozen
Clarified Butter, page 131

Heat oven to 375°. In a skillet, melt 2 tbs. butter over medium-high heat and sauté onion and mushrooms until limp; cool. Add cilantro, parsley, cumin, salt and pepper to skillet. Taste and adjust seasonings. Place 1 sheet of the phyllo on a work surface and brush with Clarified Butter. Cover with a second sheet of phyllo and brush again with butter. Cut buttered phyllo lengthwise into 3 strips. Place about 1 tbs. filling in the center on one end of each strip. Fold sides in over filling and roll up cigar fashion into a tight packet. Brush outside of packets with butter and place on a rimmed cookie sheet. Repeat with remaining ingredients. Bake packets for 20 minutes or until golden brown. Serve warm.

GREEK SPINACH AND
CHEESE PACKETS (SPANAKOPITA)

This recipe can be used as a luncheon entrée by making the pastries considerably larger. These can be frozen and brought out as needed when drop-in guests arrive. Thaw for 15 to 20 minutes before baking (you may also need to bake them for a little longer). To keep phyllo from drying out while working, cover it with a slightly damp cloth.

2 tbs. butter
½ medium onion, chopped
1 pkg. (10 oz.) frozen chopped spinach, thawed, squeezed very dry
½ tsp. nutmeg
salt and pepper to taste
½ lb. ricotta cheese
2 eggs, beaten
½ pkg. (1 lb. pkg.) phyllo dough, thawed if frozen
Clarified Butter, follows

Heat oven to 425°. In a skillet, melt 2 tbs. butter over medium heat and sauté onion until tender. Remove skillet from heat and add spinach, nutmeg, salt, pepper, ricotta and eggs; mix well and cool to room temperature. Place 1 sheet of the phyllo on a work surface and brush with Clarified Butter. Cut phyllo lengthwise into 3 strips. Place a heaping teaspoonful of spinach mixture in the top corner of each strip and fold like a flag, into a triangular bundle. Brush outside of triangles with butter and place on a rimmed cookie sheet. Repeat with remaining ingredients. Bake triangles for about 15 minutes or until golden brown. Serve warm.

CLARIFIED BUTTER

To "clarify" butter means to melt it and separate the milk solids from the golden, liquid butterfat. This allows the butter to withstand higher cooking temperatures without burning.

1/2 lb. (2 sticks) unsalted butter (no substitutes)

In a heavy saucepan, melt butter very slowly over low heat until the milk solids separate and sink to the bottom. Skim the foam that rises to the top and discard. Very carefully pour off just the golden liquid.

PESTO PARMESAN SWIRLS

These delicious appetizers take just minutes to prepare using purchased pesto and puff pastry. You can even keep them frozen until you're ready to bake (thaw before baking).

12 oz. cream cheese, softened
½ cup (2 oz.) grated Parmesan cheese
2 green onions, finely minced
¼ cup purchased pesto
1 pkg. (17¼ oz.) puff pastry sheets, thawed if frozen

In a food processor workbowl or blender container, process cream cheese, Parmesan, green onions and pesto until well blended. Lay pastry sheets on a work surface and spread with filling, dividing evenly. Roll pastry up tightly, jelly-roll fashion, starting with a long side. Wrap rolls with plastic wrap and freeze until ready to bake.

Fifteen minutes before baking, heat oven to 375° and place rolls on the counter to thaw. Cut rolls into ¼-inch rounds. Place rounds on ungreased cookie sheets and bake for 10 to 15 minutes until golden brown. Serve warm.

CRISPY CRAB ROLLS

Makes about 72 rolls

This crab-filled flaky pastry has a touch of heat. Make these far ahead of time and bake at the last minute. To keep phyllo sheets from drying out while you are working, cover them with a slightly damp cloth.

4 shallots, minced
¼ cup (½ stick) butter
2 cloves garlic, minced
½ cup chopped fresh parsley
1 tsp. dried dill weed, or more to taste

2 tbs. prepared horseradish
12 oz. crabmeat
about 1 pkg. (1 lb.) phyllo dough, thawed if frozen
Clarified Butter, page 131

Heat oven to 350°. In a skillet, sauté shallots in butter until limp; stir in garlic, parsley, dill and horseradish. Remove skillet from heat and stir in crabmeat. Taste and adjust seasonings. Place 1 sheet of the phyllo on a work surface and brush with Clarified Butter. Cut buttered phyllo lengthwise into 3 strips. Place about 1 tbs. filling in the center on one end of each strip. Fold sides in over filling and roll up cigar fashion into a tight packet. Brush outside of packets with butter and place on a rimmed cookie sheet. Repeat with remaining ingredients. Bake packets for 15 minutes or until golden brown. Serve warm.

CRAB TURNOVERS

Here, puff pastry encases a creamy dill-flavored crab mixture.

¼ cup (½ stick) butter
12 oz. mushrooms, chopped
½ cup chopped green onions
1 tsp. salt
½ tsp. pepper
1 heaping tbs. flour
12 oz. crabmeat
¼ cup sour cream

¼ cup chopped fresh parsley
1 tsp. dried dill weed
1 pkg. (10 oz.) frozen chopped spinach,
   thawed, squeezed very dry
1 pkg. (17¼ oz.) puff pastry sheets, thawed
   if frozen
1 egg, slightly beaten with 1 pinch salt
2–3 tbs. grated Parmesan cheese

Heat oven to 425°. In a skillet, melt butter over medium-high heat and sauté mushrooms and onions until soft. Add salt, pepper and flour and cook for about 30 seconds. Remove from heat and gently stir in crabmeat, sour cream, parsley and dill. Add spinach, mix well, taste and adjust seasonings. Place puff pastry on a floured work surface and cut into rounds with a 2½- to 3-inch cutter. Brush pastry rounds with egg mixture. Place 1 tbs. filling in the center of each round and sprinkle with Parmesan. Fold dough in half and crimp edges with a fork. Brush tops of turnovers with egg and prick with a fork to vent steam. Place on a cookie sheet and bake for 30 minutes or until golden brown. Serve warm.

BRIE IN PUFF PASTRY

This recipe's beautiful presentation is made easy by using packaged puff pastry. It should ideally be served with either fruit or crackers.

2 small wheels (2.2 lb. each) Brie cheese
1 pkg. (17¼ oz.) puff pastry sheets, thawed
  if frozen

1 egg yolk
1 tbs. cold water
1 pinch salt

Place puff pastry sheets on a work surface. Using the Brie container or Brie wheel as a guide, cut 4 circles from the puff pastry. Sandwich each Brie wheel between 2 rounds of puff pastry. Cut remaining pastry into 1-inch strips and press on sides of Brie. Crimp edges of pastry together so that Brie wheels are completely enclosed. Place pastry-covered wheels on a rimmed cookie sheet. In a small bowl, beat egg yolk with water and salt and brush over the top and sides of pastry shell. Cut decorative shapes from any remaining pastry, if desired, and place on top of cheese wheels. Brush again with yolk mixture. Refrigerate until ready to bake.

Just before serving, heat oven to 450°. Bake cheese rounds for 10 minutes. Reduce oven heat to 350° and continue baking for 20 minutes. Pastry should be puffed and golden brown. Cool for at least 15 minutes before serving. Serve warm or at room temperature.

HONEY LAMB PUFFS

These Middle Eastern delights have a very satisfying, piquant quality.

¼ cup raisins
1 cup hot water
¼ cup olive oil
1¾ cups finely chopped onions
1 tbs. minced garlic
1 lb. ground lamb
2 tsp. salt
1½ tsp. pepper

1 tsp. cinnamon
⅛ tsp. cayenne pepper
¼ cup tomato paste
1 cup chopped fresh tomatoes
⅓ cup honey
1 pkg. (17¼ oz.) puff pastry sheets, thawed
    if frozen

Heat oven to 375°. Soak raisins in hot water until plump, about 30 minutes; drain. In a large skillet, heat olive oil over medium heat and sauté onions and garlic until tender. Add lamb, salt, pepper, cinnamon and cayenne and sauté until meat is no longer pink. Add tomato paste, tomatoes, raisins and honey to skillet and simmer for several minutes; taste and adjust seasonings. Cool filling to room temperature. Place pastry on a work surface and cut each sheet into 16 squares. Line miniature muffin tins with pastry squares and place about 2 tsp. filling in each pastry-lined cup. Bake for about 20 minutes or until golden brown. Serve warm or at room temperature.

PUFF PASTRY PORK SWIRLS

Make this very tasty, easy-to-make recipe far in advance and freeze it. It can be made in bulk for large parties.

1 pkg. (17¼ oz.) frozen puff pastry sheets, thawed until just pliable
1 lb. ground pork
2 tsp. ground cumin
1 tsp. dried thyme
1 tbs. minced garlic
¼ cup finely chopped green onions
¼ cup finely chopped red bell pepper or pimiento
salt and pepper to taste
1 egg, slightly beaten with pinch salt

On a lightly floured work surface, roll pastry to ⅛-inch thick. Cut crosswise into 3-inch-wide strips. Place strips on cookie sheets that have been sprayed with cold water and refrigerate. In a bowl, mix pork with cumin, thyme, garlic, onions, bell pepper, salt and pepper. Spread pork mixture over pastry strips, dividing evenly. Brush dough edges with water and roll up tightly, jelly roll-fashion, starting with long side. Refrigerate or freeze until ready to bake.

Fifteen minutes before baking, heat oven to 375° and place rolls on the counter to thaw, if necessary. Cut rolls into ½-inch rounds. Place rounds on ungreased cookie sheets, brush with egg mixture and bake for about 15 minutes, until golden brown. Serve warm.

CHICKEN EMPANADAS

Makes about 24 empanadas

This delicious Mexican treat is easy to make when you use purchased puff pastry. If you prefer a spicier mixture, increase the amount of pepper flakes.

⅓ cup raisins
1 cup hot water
3 tbs. vegetable oil
⅔ cup minced onion
1 lb. diced raw chicken
¾ tsp. red pepper flakes, or more to taste
1½ tsp. salt
¼ tsp. cinnamon
1 tsp. ground cumin

2 tbs. butter
2 tbs. flour
1 cup chicken stock
3 tbs. chopped green olives
1 pkg. (17¼ oz.) puff pastry sheets, thawed if frozen
1 egg, beaten
3 tbs. toasted slivered almonds

Soak raisins in hot water until plump, about 30 minutes; drain. In a skillet, heat oil over medium heat and sauté onion until soft. Add chicken, pepper flakes, salt, cinnamon and cumin and sauté for 5 minutes. In a small saucepan, melt butter over medium heat and stir in flour until smooth. Add chicken stock and cook, stirring, until thickened. Add stock mixture to chicken mixture with raisins and green olives, stir well and cool to room temperature.

Heat oven to 375°. Place puff pastry on a floured work surface and roll out to ⅛-inch thick. Cut pastry into rounds with a 3-inch cutter. Place a small amount of filling in the center of each round, dividing evenly. Brush dough edges with water, fold in half to enclose filling and crimp edges with a fork. Place empanadas on a lightly greased cookie sheet, brush with egg and sprinkle with toasted almonds. Bake for 20 to 30 minutes or until golden brown. Serve warm.

SAUSAGE IN BRIOCHE

Great for picnics or boating, this is traditionally served on Bibb lettuce and accompanied by gherkin pickles and Dijon mustard. It goes well with soups and salads.

1 pkg. active dry yeast
3 tbs. warm milk
2 tsp. sugar
½ cup (1 stick) butter, cut into pieces
2 cups flour
1 tsp. salt

2 eggs
1 cooked 6- to 7-inch sausage, about 2
   inches in diameter, ends trimmed
1 egg yolk
1 tsp. water
1 pinch salt

In a food processor workbowl, mix yeast with milk and sugar and let stand for 5 minutes. Add butter, flour, salt and eggs to workbowl and process for 3 minutes. Transfer dough to an oiled bowl and slash top with an X. Cover with plastic wrap and let rise in a warm, draft-free place until doubled in bulk, about 45 minutes.

Heat oven to 400°. Punch down dough and form into a 10-x-8-inch rectangle. Place sausage in middle of dough and encase with dough, crimping dough edges together securely. Transfer dough-encased sausage to a greased baking pan. Mix egg yolk with water and salt and brush over the surface of dough. Bake for 35 minutes, until golden brown. Cool for 10 minutes. Cut into 12 slices.

BAKED VEGETABLE AND CHICKEN WON TONS Makes 24 won tons

Won ton wrappers are fat-free and serve as a good, but less flaky, alternative to puff pastry or buttered phyllo. Serve with purchased sweet and sour sauce, plum sauce or even teriyaki sauce.

½ lb. ground chicken or turkey
¼ cup chopped celery
½ cup shredded carrots
1 tbs. dry sherry
2 tsp. grated fresh ginger

1 tbs. soy sauce
2 tsp. cornstarch
⅓ cup purchased plum sauce or sweet and
    sour sauce
24 square won ton wrappers

Heat oven to 375°. In a nonstick skillet over medium-high heat, sauté chicken with celery and carrots for several minutes. Stir in sherry, ginger, soy sauce, cornstarch and plum sauce. Remove skillet from heat and cool filling to room temperature. Place won ton wrappers on a work surface and moisten edges with water. Place a rounded teaspoonful of filling in the center of each wrapper and pinch opposite ends together to seal. Spray a cookie sheet with nonstick cooking spray. Place filled won tons on cookie sheet and spray won tons lightly with cooking spray. Bake for about 10 minutes or until brown and crisp. Serve warm.

RUSSIAN MEAT TURNOVERS (PIROSHKI)

This traditional Russian favorite can be made ahead and frozen; thaw frozen pastries before baking. Instead of sandwiches for your next picnic, make extra-large piroshki by cutting large rounds out of the pastry.

1 cup plus 3 tbs. butter, softened, divided
1 cup plus 2 tbs. sour cream, divided
2½ cups flour
1 tsp. salt
2 medium onions, finely chopped
1 lb. lean ground beef
¼ cup cooked rice

1 tbs. dried dill weed
¼ cup chopped fresh parsley
1 tsp. salt
½ tsp. pepper
2 hard-cooked eggs, chopped
1 egg beaten with 1 tsp. water

In a bowl, mix 1 cup of the butter with 1 cup of the sour cream until blended; stir in flour and salt until a smooth dough forms. Form dough into a ball, wrap with plastic wrap and refrigerate for 2 hours.

Heat oven to 400°. In a skillet, heat remaining 3 tbs. butter over medium-high heat and sauté onions until golden brown. Add beef and sauté until meat is no longer pink. Remove skillet from heat and drain off fat. Add remaining 2 tbs. sour cream, rice, dill, parsley, salt, pepper and hard-cooked eggs to skillet and stir until well mixed; cool to room temperature. On a lightly floured work surface, roll dough out to ⅛-inch thick. Cut dough into rounds with a 3-inch cutter. Place a small amount of filling in the center of each round, dividing evenly. Brush dough edges with water, fold dough in half and crimp edges with a fork. Place turnovers on a lightly greased cookie sheet and brush with beaten egg. Bake for 15 to 20 minutes or until golden brown. Serve warm.

CHINESE PORK DUMPLINGS (POT STICKERS)

These are common "dim sum," the Chinese word for appetizer.

2 tsp. minced fresh ginger
2 green onions, finely minced
6 tbs. cream sherry, divided
1 lb. ground pork
2 tbs. soy sauce
1 tsp. salt
¼ tsp. pepper
1 tsp. sugar

3 tbs. toasted sesame oil, divided
½ cup chopped water chestnuts
1 tbs. chopped fresh cilantro
30 round won ton wrappers
3 tbs. vegetable oil
1 tbs. white vinegar
1 cup water

Soak ginger and green onions in 4 tbs. of the sherry; let stand for 10 minutes and drain. Place mixture in a bowl with pork, soy sauce, salt, pepper, sugar, 1 tbs. of the sesame oil, water chestnuts and cilantro and mix well. Place won ton wrappers on a work surface and moisten edges with water. Place 2 tsp. filling in the center of each wrapper and fold in half. Pleat or crimp edges together. Heat vegetable oil in an extra-large skillet, arrange dumplings in circles, cover and cook over medium heat for 3 minutes. Combine remaining sherry and sesame oil with vinegar and water, add to skillet and cook uncovered until liquid is absorbed.

BLACK-EYED SUSANS

Sweet dates encased in a cheese pastry are a Southern specialty.

1 cup (2 sticks) cold butter, cut into small cubes
4 cups (1 lb.) shredded sharp cheddar cheese
2 cups flour
1 pinch salt
1 pinch cayenne pepper, or more to taste
1 lb. pitted dates
½ cup sugar

Heat oven to 300°. In a food processor workbowl or in a bowl with a pastry blender, quickly mix butter, cheese, flour, salt and cayenne until a dough forms. Shape dough into 36 to 48 balls. Press a date into the center of each ball, encasing it entirely with dough. Roll balls in sugar and place on a cookie sheet. Bake for about 30 minutes. Cool on a rack.

OLIVE PUFFS

Green olives are encased in cheese pastry and served warm. Keep a large quantity of these in the freezer so you won't run out. Thaw them before baking.

2 cups (8 oz.) shredded sharp cheddar cheese
½ cup (1 stick) butter, softened
1 cup flour
36 pimiento-stuffed green olives

Heat oven to 400°. In a bowl with a mixer, beat cheese, butter and flour until well mixed. Shape dough into 36 equal-sized balls. Press an olive into the center of each ball, encasing it entirely with dough. Place balls on a cookie sheet and bake for 20 minutes or until golden brown.

PARTY MENU SUGGESTIONS

The following appetizer menu ideas are just suggestions and you certainly don't have to use all of the recipes. When creating your own menus, remember to use a variety of dishes, an assortment of textures, and, if possible, a mixture of hot and cold dishes. It's also nice to provide vegetarian and low-fat selections for your guests and something refreshing and sweet, such as a fresh fruit dish.

ELEGANT APPETIZER BUFFET

Creamy Crab Spread, page 64
Marinated Grilled Shrimp, page 113
Brie in Wine Aspic, page 54
Smoked Salmon Treats, page 85

French Caviar Potatoes, page 99
Bacon-Stuffed Cherry Tomatoes, page 72
Spiced Melon Balls, page 16
Curried Cashews, page 18

BABY OR WEDDING SHOWER

Cheesy Crab Toast, page 11
Warm Cheese Wafers, page 97
Fruit Kabobs, page 90
Date Bread with Pineapple Cream Cheese,
   page 82

Lattice Cream Cheese Mold, page 56
Olive Spread (Tapenade), page 44
Miniature French Quiches, page 100
Sweet and Sour Pupus, page 125

BIG GAME PARTY

Barbeque Chicken Wings, page 116
Sweet and Sour Meatballs, page 122
Smoked Turkey Rolls, page 83
Hoisin Spareribs, page 124

Pesto Mushrooms, page 106
Crunchy Ham and Cheese Ball, page 62
Guacamole, page 29

HOLIDAY CELEBRATION

Sweet and Savory Stuffed Brie, page 53
Teriyaki Chicken Skewers, page 118
Marinated Olives, page 9
Black-Eyed Susans, page 145

Crispy Crab Rolls, page 133
Low-fat Salmon Mousse, page 67
Baked Clams, page 114
Simple Liver Paté, page 58
Gorgonzola Spread, page 49

VEGETARIAN DELIGHT

Smoky Eggplant Dip (Baba Ghanoush),
    page 33
Chutney-Stuffed Celery, page 69
Sweet Potato and Carrot Dip, page 31

Smoky Cheese Fondue, page 37
Hot Garlic and Anchovy Dip, page 34
Garbanzo Bean Dip (Hummus), page 32
Cucumber-Herb Canapés, page 76

LOW-FAT APPETIZER PARTY

Honey Chicken Wings, page 117
Eggplant Antipasto (Caponata), page 46
Spinach-Stuffed Mushrooms, page 108
Marinated Asparagus or Cauliflower,
    page 14

Stuffed Grape Leaves, page 70
Low-fat Cucumber Dip, page 27
Baked Vegetable and Chicken Won Tons,
    page 141

FESTIVE PICNIC

LIGHT BRUNCH

MAKE AHEAD APPETIZER PARTY

COCKTAIL PARTY

Mushroom Phyllo Tarts, page 105
Pesto Parmesan Swirls, page 132
*Goat Cheese, Pesto and Sun-Dried Tomato
   Terrine,* page 52
Cucumber-Herb Canapés, page 76
Teriyaki Mixed Nuts, page 19

Cheese Straws, page 21
Middle Eastern Vegetable Packets, page 129
Sesame Walnut Chicken Strips, page 120
Creamy Stuffed Dates, page 91
Brie in Puff Pastry, page 135

TEA PARTY

*Strawberries Stuffed with Orange Cream
   Cheese,* page 89
Pumpkin Tea Sandwiches, page 80
Marbled Tea Eggs, page 74
Cucumber-Mint Coolers, page 77
Olive Puffs, page 146

Shrimp Salad Puffs, page 86
Crab Fondue, page 38
Roquefort Mousse, page 50
Three-Cheese Phyllo with Walnuts,
   page 128

INDEX

Serve Creative, Easy, Nutritious Meals with nitty gritty® Cookbooks

1 or 2, Cooking for
100 Dynamite Desserts
9 x 13 Pan Cookbook
Bagels, Best
Barbecue Cookbook
Beer and Good Food
Blender Drinks
Bread Baking
Bread Machine
Bread Machine II
Bread Machine III
Bread Machine V
Bread Machine VI
Bread Machine, Entrees
Burger Bible
Cappuccino/Espresso
Casseroles
Chicken, Unbeatable
Chile Peppers
Clay, Cooking in
Coffee and Tea
Convection Oven

Cook-Ahead Cookbook
Crockery Pot, Extra-Special
Deep Fryer
Dehydrator Cookbook
Edible Gifts
Edible Pockets
Fabulous Fiber Cookery
Fondue and Hot Dips
Fondue, New International
Fresh Vegetables
Freezer, 'Fridge, Pantry
Garlic Cookbook
Grains, Cooking with
Healthy Cooking on Run
Ice Cream Maker
Indoor Grill, Cooking on
Italian Recipes
Juicer Book II
Kids, Cooking with Your
Kids, Healthy Snacks for
Loaf Pan, Recipes for
Low-Carb Recipes

Lowfat American
No Salt No Sugar No Fat
Party Foods/Appetizers
Pasta Machine Cookbook
Pasta, Quick and Easy
Pinch of Time
Pizza, Best
Porcelain, Cooking in
Pressure Cooker, Recipes
Rice Cooker
Rotisserie Oven Cooking
Sandwich Maker
Simple Substitutions
Skillet, Sensational
Slow Cooking
Slow Cooker, Vegetarian
Soups and Stews
Soy & Tofu Recipes
Tapas Fantásticas
Toaster Oven Cookbook
Waffles & Pizzelles
Wraps and Roll-Ups

For a free catalog, call: Bristol Publishing Enterprises
(800) 346-4889
www.bristolpublishing.com